Loan Officer Freedom

How to Get More Closings
While Doing Only the Things You Love to Do

Carl White

FREE – Strategy Call

This Book Includes a Free Strategy Call You Can
Use RIGHT NOW to Get off the Sales Rollercoaster.

Get It NOW at
www.LoanOfficerStrategyCall.com

MORTGAGE MARKETING ANIMALS

Published by
Mortgage Marketing Animals

Copyright ©2021 The Marketing Animals
Printed in the United States of America

ISBN: 978-1-7324655-4-1

Mortgage Marketing Animals
Palm Harbor, FL
MortgageMarketingAnimals.com

Dedication

This being my fourth book, the "who" question
on the dedication jumped out at me.

My dearest mother, Joan White, not only made it possible for me
to have my first breath and the gift of life itself but she also gifted
me with the hunger for knowledge.

As a wee lad, she would take me to the library every Sunday
to pick out a couple of books to bring home. These books would
take me to foreign lands, solving mysteries, and experiencing
wondrous journeys, all while teaching me the gift of knowledge
and learning how to leverage that power.

I never would have dreamed that, one day, I would write books
of my own, much less that I would have multiple best sellers.
It's truly surreal.

I trust she knows the impact this has made in my life.
It's been immense.

So Mother, this book is dedicated to you. I'm forever grateful.

And now I hope to help you, reader, at some level… to impact
your life by sharing the knowledge I now have that I wish
I would have had 20 years ago when I entered this amazing
business of being a loan officer.

Now, onward to YOUR wondrous journey….

Foreword by Barry Habib

There is only one thing we cannot produce more of… *Time*. It is
truly the most valuable commod-
ity. And maximizing what you
do with the time you have can be
the difference between extreme
success and something far less.

There is a big distinction
between being busy and being
productive. In the pages that fol-
low, my good friend Carl White will help you be far more productive instead of just busy.

I have known Carl for many years as a great leader and influ-
encer in the mortgage space. The success stories from Carl's
coaching and training are too many to number, but there is a con-
sistent theme—Carl teaches you with heart, integrity, and proven
systems that generate results. All you need to do is follow along.

In this book, Carl will help you identify the activities that give
you a greater return for the cost of your time and how to minimize
the activities that don't give you the desired return, all while con-
tinuing to be effective in all areas. Once identified, you will learn
how to maximize those high-yielding activities so that you can
increase your income and success.

Freeing up time will clearly increase your income, but more importantly, it will also improve your quality of life. Carl is not suggesting you use all your time towards work… it is actually the opposite. Carl will teach you how to work fewer hours, while earning more, so you can spend more time doing things you love to do.

I enjoyed reading this book because it speaks to something that we all desire more of—*Time*. Remember that this is *your* time. And your time is now.

>   —Barry Habib
>   CEO of MBS Highway
>   Crystal Ball Award Winner (2018, 2020)
>   2019 Mortgage Professional of the Year
>   (*National Mortgage Professional* magazine)

Note from the Author

Carl White

I decided that a done book was better than a perfect one so you might find spelling, grammar and layout mistakes in it. If you find an error, will you do me a favor and say what you find by sending an email to **carl.white@themarketinganimals.com**?

Just note the page number, sentence and mistake so my team and I can get that fixed right away and send you a gift for your help. If you know me at all, you know I'm all about results—helping you with tools, ideas and strategies that make you money—and I live what I preach. So please help me make it better as you read it.

If you DON'T like it, send me an email, say why and I'll give you your money back, ok? I don't want your money if you're not thrilled with what you get out of this book. No matter what, I will consider us friends.

Thanks again for your support… now get ready to get off the Sales Rollercoaster by closing more deals doing only what you love to do!

Table of Contents

Endorsements and Kudos

"I don't think I'd get to be where I'm at today if it weren't for the people of Freedom Club sharing their energy, values, and ideas, and methods with each other..."

—Scott Griffin

"I've received so much encouragement and guidance on so many levels...life coaching, business coaching, and financial coaching and I've found the coaches at The Mortgage Marketing Animals to be my family, I've received so much value from all of them. They are phenomenal!"

—Colleen Wood

"When I joined The Freedom Club I was working upwards of 60–80 hours a week... [now] my work week is a normal 35–40 hours and I don't touch my computer until after I drop my kids to school. The change has been amazing. My kids will certainly know work ethic but more important they have their mom back and they know that they are my priorities!"

—Toni Taylor

"Since joining MMA I am finally gaining traction on Realtors and lead generation. I feel like I have the direction now that I was missing in an executable game plan.

- *Facebook Messenger campaign — netted 14 Realtor Zoom appointments. Most said they would send their next deal my way.*
- *I made each new Realtor a co-branded mobile app for easy sharing with prospects for prequalifying.*
- *Another Realtor is working on her personal purchase and is not happy with her current loan officer — if the appraisal hasn't closed, she is swinging it my way.*
- *Past database calls on one of my declines from two years ago came in today and I am reviewing refinancing on four of her properties.*
- *I have my first Loan Partner interview*
- *I counted 160 contacts using phone, text or video over the last two weeks and I can feel the momentum. I am actually more productive going Mach 4 with my hair on fire.*
- *I got two Realtors to send me a video — they were terrified to do so but they did it anyway!*

The morning show has inspired me and I finally feel like I am getting on top of this. I dig listening to it during my work out and implementing all the ideas. I'm looking forward to learning about the Agent Mastermind. Thanks for the guidance and leadership!"

—Mike Henson

Introduction

No Limits

A lot of loan officers have an issue with what I call the 'Sales Rollercoaster'. The purpose of this book is to get you off that wild ride by showing you how to get more closings while doing only the things you love to do.

The important thing about only doing what you love to do means there is no limitation on your growth. The only time you limit your growth is when you get some reward, like more money, but have to do something you don't enjoy doing to get that reward. When that happens, you will want to limit doing that activity. In this case, that means you are limiting your income because more money means doing more of that thing you don't want to do.

The key to having a successful mortgage business is only doing those activities that you LOVE doing, that you are really good at and that make you money. We call this the Triad of Awesomeness. This eliminates burn-out so there is no limitation on your income.

Burn-out happens when you're doing something you don't like doing for an extended period of time. You do it because you get a benefit, but the process of getting that benefit stinks.

Now that doesn't mean that particular activity is a bad activity! It just means that it's a bad activity for YOU and maybe somebody else can handle that for you. But I'm getting ahead of myself here… we will go into more detail about this later in the book.

A little 'fine' print before we go further… (and maybe it's not all that fine—ha!).

The Fine Print

I'm not an attorney. Nor are there any attorneys involved in writing any part of this book. So as you read this book, make sure anything you do is compliant for your state, your company and RESPA (the Real Estate Settlement Procedures Act).

You should know I'm not going to talk about anything even remotely risqué or edgy. As a branch manager for one of the largest branches in the nation, we've run what I'm going to be sharing with you through our compliance attorney and gotten the green light. But just like two different accountants could give you two different tax returns, you'll want to run what you do through your company attorney to make sure you're in compliance where needed.

All I'm going to share in this book is what we're doing in my branch as well as what some other top producers who are part of the Freedom Club (an elite private group of top producing loan officers and branch managers) are doing to get off the Sales Rollercoaster, all while having epic increases in their business, you know, "mo money". None of this stuff is theory or "gee, that seems like a good idea"—this is activity we are actually doing in my branch or that others are actively doing in their businesses. It's road-tested and proven to get results.

What to Expect from This Book

This substance of this book will be delivered both here and then continued in various online events and the Marketing Animals Community so you take what you learn here further. My intention is you have resources when and as you need them.

First, we have to take stuff off your plate before we put more stuff on it. How many times have you gotten new great ideas by reading a book or going to a seminar and then after you've finished it, nothing gets done? Look, we all have and it's totally not your fault. The reason why you haven't taken additional action is because your plate is already full. You have to decide what activity will get reduced, eliminated, automated or delegated and, at the same time, you need to decide what items will stay on your to do list.

The priority is to help you decide what to clear off your plate so you can start doing more loan-getting activities—which means working on the single thing that makes you the most money AND that you enjoy doing. We'll cover who you'll need on your team, who does what, we'll show you the perfect file flow for your championship team—which is the same file flow we follow in my branch.

The second part of this book series, due to be released about six months from this one, will get specific about the activities that top loan officers and branch managers do each day of the week to bring more loans in the door with zero cold calling. Not that there's anything wrong with cold calling—it's just not going to be our first choice (or second or third). There are other faster and more effective ways.

A Strategic "Brain Dump"

Basically, these books are a "Brain Dump". If you're not familiar with what that is, it's one of my favorite things to do. Several times a year, 10 to 15 of us fly in from all over the country and then spend eight hours "dumping" our best ideas for our businesses. It's a very powerful activity.

Each person shares for 10 to 15 minutes what's really working for them. By the time you hear all these great ideas, you might be able to match ideas from the first person with the third person and come up with a whole new strategy. It's like one plus one equals FIFTY! And that's what I'm going to be doing here… sharing as much as I can to help you get off the Sales Rollercoaster.

Three things I do want to make sure we cover in this first book are:

1. Always wear black pants,
2. This is a perverted industry (although not in a way you might think), and,
3. Curly from City Slickers.

Stay tuned for that.

As you begin to read this book, I am going to be sharing some real life numbers and results for my branch and for some of my private coaching members. Please don't get overwhelmed and think it can't happen to you. You might think *"well, Carl is doing those numbers but there's no way I can do that"*, or *"Bob is producing all those loans but I can't"* or *"I see Susie closing all those loans but there's no way I can do it."* We all started at the same place—zero! We all have been where you are now; it's just some of us have just been paddling up the river a little bit longer. So start thinking, *"If Carl can do it, so can I!"*

In fact, let me share something that changed the direction of my life.

Little Guy

I tell a story at my events about when I lived in Hampton, VA, many moons ago. I won't tell you the whole story now (you'll just have to come to an event to hear it) but I will tell you the result of it.

I came to a crossroad in my life where I could either go to college (and for someone who barely graduated high school, can you say SCARY???) or I could stay stuck in the party lifestyle that was quickly becoming my "norm."

I chose college but, for me, it was a HUGE leap of faith. This internal beast I named "Little Guy" kept popping up on my shoulder telling me I wasn't good enough, I wasn't smart enough, I didn't have what it takes and I didn't deserve it. We wrestled every single day!

With the help of my family (particularly my Uncle David), I

made daily decisions to kick "Little Guy" to the curb and keep moving forward. As a result of that daily choice, I met my beautiful bride, got my honors degree in the Sciences (of all things!) and had an amazing career for close to 10 years in the medical field. I later found it didn't feed my soul so I made the jump to the Mortgage World, but I never forgot the lesson it taught me.

Do You Have a "Little Guy"?

We all have something—some saboteur, some false belief—we have to battle. I still fight with him but I've gotten really good at shutting him down. If Little Guy/Gal gets on your shoulder, trying to tell you all the reasons you can't do something, make a simple decision to flick Little Guy off your shoulder. Because today is your day. If I can do it, so can you.

Who Am I and Why Should You Listen to Or Trust Me

The team I put together funded over $700M last year (average loan amount around $187,000). A slow, slow month for us this year is around 400 loans for the month. This year (2020), we have already had a month where we closed over 743 loans in just one month. I'm honored to be part of such an amazing team.

Even more surprising to you might be the fact that I do what I do while working less than 32 hours a week. I typically work Monday through Thursday from 9:00ish to 5:00. I also take around six vacations per year (one or two of them is usually a three-week vacation to other countries). I do this by following the team-building principles I'll show you in this book.

I think it's critically important we work like this not just because it's good for our family life and our own well-being, but because we get more productivity by working, at most, a 32-hour work week. Think of your work, of you, like a racehorse. If we were going to send a racehorse to the Kentucky Derby, would we race them every single day right before the race? Or would we run them for a bit and then let them rest a couple of days? And then run them for a bit again? You have to do that interval training to rebuild reserves. If a racehorse needs to do that, who are we to think we don't need that same kind of recovery time to build our capacity?

A friend of mine is a professor at the University of North Carolina in Chapel Hill. She did some studies that show we are most productive with a 32-hour work week. Working more hours produced less results per hour and less overall total results. We maximize our output at 32 hours a week.

I love having time in the morning to get ready for my day. I LOVE being able to ride my bike and listen to podcasts and sip hot tea with my lovely bride every morning and then relax and eat dinner, then go for a walk with her every night. And if you farm stuff out, delegate things you don't like, and you focus only on the highest-producing activities, you don't have to get in to work before 9 A.M. to get stuff done. You get stuff done between 9 and 5 with very little interruption.

Lowest Paid "Per Loan"

Now even though I've made many millions of dollars over the years in the mortgage business, and even though I got paid on somewhere around $700M in loan production last year, and certainly over $1 billion in production just this year alone, there probably aren't too many people who make less "per loan" than I do. Despite this, I still may very well be the highest-paid person you know in the industry. I think it is because I have a "watermelon" mentality. Here's what I mean.

Instead of getting 100% of a grape, I'd rather get 50% of a watermelon. Heck, even 25% of a watermelon is still more than 100% of a grape!!! Everything I'm going to show you takes an investment, often in people, technology and systems. I cannot tell you how many people I've seen go after the proverbial grape. And even though they are getting 100% of that grape, they could be getting 50% of a watermelon. It's the number one biggest mistake I see people make in their business. It's not how many BPS you make, it's what you put in your pocket at the end of the day as well as your "Coolness Factor."

Elevate Your Coolness Factor

Before we get too far into this, I want to make sure we cover this one thing that's especially important. One of the things I'm known for in the mortgage industry is helping loan officers elevate their Coolness Factor. In this case, it's about helping YOU elevate YOUR Coolness Factor. This is actually a mathematical equation. Think back to your school days and fractions. Here is the equation:

$$\text{Coolness Factor} = \text{Income} / \text{Stress}$$

In this fraction, if we increase income (numerator) but then increase stress (denominator) proportionately—the Coolness Factor doesn't change. In simple math, if your income is three and your stress is three, and we increase your income to six and your stress to six, your Coolness Factor—your happiness level—doesn't change. This is why a lot of people who are very wealthy are also very unhappy.

What I'm known for (and what this book is going to talk about) is how to *increase* income and *decrease* stress. Because if you increase income and then decrease stress, your Coolness Factor goes up—WAY up. For example, if your income goes from six to twenty, and your stress goes from five down to one, we've drastically increased your Coolness Factor. This in turn will make an epic difference in your mortgage business.

Let's talk about what freedom looks like next.

Chapter 1

3 Kinds of Freedom

There are three kinds of freedom we're going to talk about in this book.

1. Financial Freedom: having all the money to do what you want to do.
2. Time Freedom: having the time to do those things that Financial Freedom has given you.
3. Relationship Freedom: spending your time and money with who you want which, in turn, leads to less stress.

I've had each of these three freedoms separate from each other. I've had time freedom but not financial freedom and relationship freedom but no financial or time freedom. One without the other two is no good. Two without the other one is no good. You have got to get all three of these freedoms to truly live what I call an epic life.

In other words, you want to design a business that is your servant, not your master.

The good thing about being a loan officer is we don't sell pencils for a living. What I mean by that is somebody who sells pencils for a living makes something like a penny per pencil. We don't do that.

As a rough rule of thumb (and for really easy math), we are going to say the average loan officer makes about $2,000 per closing. Now I understand some loan officers might be significantly lower ($500-1000 per closing) or significantly higher ($8-10,000 per closing). But for the purpose of this book, let's just use $2,000… that's an average loan amount of $200K making 100bps.

The Power of an Extra $12,000 Per Month

So if I help you increase your business by just an extra six loans a month, it could give you a $12,000 per month raise, which is an extra $144,000 per year! And that's with just increasing by five more loans a month. We've seen that happen really easily. That's a major difference we can make with our programs. Now, that's not all we want you to do, of course, but hey—every $144,000 helps, right?

As LOs, We Don't Sell Pencils...

Each additional loan brings you in an extra

$1,500   ($2,000) $3,500

**So increasing your business by an extra 6 loans
per month could give you a $12,000 per month raise of
an Extra $144,000 per year!!!**

What would an extra $10K a month do for you and your family? A new car? A new house? New toys? Private school? College? A wedding? Cool vacations?

Personally, while I enjoy the things listed above, my favorite investment has been getting domestic help. I find having somebody help me in my home is so nice. It's been a relationship saver too! Now me and the lovely Mrs. White can enjoy one another instead of wondering whose turn it is to wash the dishes, vacuum the floor, or do the laundry.

How Rich People Think

One of the best things you can do as you go through this book is to change your mindset and to start thinking like the 'uber wealthy' do.

They don't ask "What will it cost me to do that?" Instead, they ask, "What will it cost me *NOT* to do that?"

Some people might say, *"gee, if I go hire someone to help me, that could cost me $4,000 a month!"* My argument would be, *"what if that person (who costs you $4,000 a month) helped you bring in another six closings?"* Six times $2,000 is $12,000; so you're investing $4,000 to make $12,000.

I always know when I'm talking to a high-level person when they ask, *"what is the yield on that?"* The yield is simply knowing the cost, knowing the return and then calculating the difference between those two. For me, if I spend $10 for something and it only produces me $5, that costs me way too much. But if I spend $4,000 to do something and it brings me $12,000, that's the deal of a lifetime. I will wear that machine OUT!! I will put those $4,000 bills in there as fast as I can to get more of the $12,000 in return.

To run a successful mortgage business, you need to write small checks to cash big checks.

Real Estate Agent Referral Partners

I want so badly for you to get value from this book that I'm going to keep rolling on how you can grow your business even BEFORE we get into the meat of this book! So let's talk about going to work with real estate agents as referral partners.

Let's say you are working my new 32-hour work week. That's 128 work hours per month. And if, in that 128 hours, I can help you bring in just ONE new real estate agent referral partner, that could be a game-changer.

We're talking one new agent per month—not ten, not five, just ONE—and if those 12 agents (remember, you are adding one new agent per month) each send you just one new deal per month, you just gave yourself a $288,000 raise!

Let's back it up to do the math… each deal brings you about $2,000. So each agent who brings you a new deal per month is creating $24,000 of income per year. And $24,000 times 12 months is a $288,000 increase per year in your income. Really.

We'll be talking about how to bring in these new agents. But, first, we have to get stuff off your plate or you're not going to be able to do it.

If you're currently closing 3–4 loans a month, it might be possible to double your business without getting help. But think about it—you'd have twice as many leads, twice as many applications, twice as many credit pulls, twice as many conditions, twice as many fires, twice as many update calls, and have to go to twice as many closings. So maybe you could double. But could you triple?? It's likely you're already working 8-10 hours a day. You can't work 16 hours a day and do that for an extended period of time. So we have to take stuff off your plate so you can grow your business.

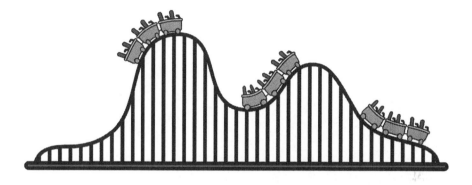

If you don't get help, you'll be on what I call the 'loan officer rollercoaster'— where you're up a month, then down a month, then up a month, then down a month, up a month, down a month. The ups are kind of cool but the downs can be very scary.

So we're going to eliminate the loan officer rollercoaster here in the next couple of pages.

Chapter 2

The Loan Officer Rollercoaster

Here's what the Loan Officer Rollercoaster looks like... we have one set of activities that builds our business called Activity A, and then another set of activities which closes that business called Activity B. Activity A is the process of bringing new loans in (prospecting, marketing, meeting with referral partners, making

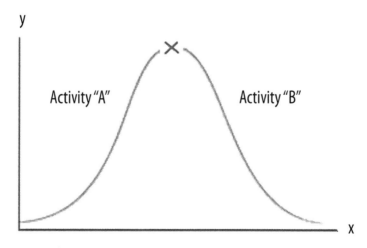

The LO Rollercoaster

sales calls, etc.); Activity B is getting those loans to close (collecting docs, running DU, disclosing the loan, putting out fires, chasing conditions, submitting to processing and underwriting, etc.) which is a whole different kind of activity.

In the life of a typical loan officer, there comes a point where they have to stop doing Activity A (loan getting) and start doing Activity B (loan closings). To grow your business, you have to figure out how you can do more of Activity A and less of Activity B. This seems like really simple stuff, right?

What If . . . ?

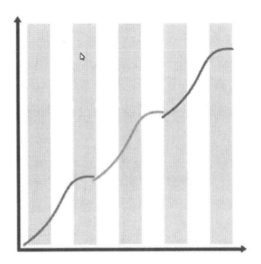

What if we could stack Activity A on top of Activity A on top of Activity A? This is what true growth looks like.

A friend of mine, James Wedmore, gave me eight words that totally changed my life. He said, "*Carl, the less I do, the more I make.*" In other words, the less of Activity B he does, the more time he has for Activity A which means more money in less time and less effort!

Now you might think, *"wait a minute, that sounds like a fairy tale."* But think of a stick shift car… by the time you hit fifth gear, you're going much faster than when in first gear yet the engine is working less. The average car gets better gas mileage in fifth gear going 50 mph rather than in first gear going 20 mph. So it works less and goes faster or, in our case, makes more money.

When identifying what our Activity A's and Activity B's are, we also have to look at Pareto's Law of Distribution. In a nutshell, this is the 80/20 Rule—80% of the wealth is produced by 20% of the population, or 80% of the loans are closed by 20% of the loan officers or 80% of our income comes from 20% of our activities.

We could even say that 80% of our headaches come from 20% of our clients, staff or referral partners. So take a few moments and identify what your "20%" is that gives you the 80% result. Which leads us straight into our next section—you still have to like what you are doing.

The Triad of Awesomeness

We teach a concept we call the Triad of Awesomeness. It's the two or three activities you LOVE doing, that you happen to be really good at AND which make you a boatload of money.

As an exercise, grab some paper and make three columns. In column one, list all the things you love doing in your mortgage business. In column two, list all the things that you are really good at. And in column three, list all the things that truly make you money.

This Is Your 20% — The TOA

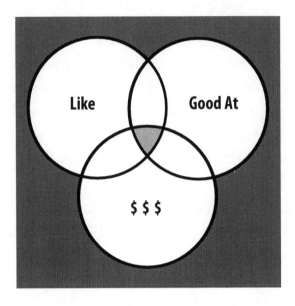

Then look at the very small percentage of items—maybe two, three or four at the max—that fall into all three categories. Those few things will intersect and form a triangle in the center, and we call that the TOA, or the Triangle of Awesomeness.

Typically, the money is not made in the "paperwork" side of our business. Things like chasing paperwork, structuring the deal, putting out fires or taking the perfect application (all absolutely necessary) isn't what makes you the money; instead, it's bringing the loans in, bringing the leads in (SALES ACTIVITIES) where the money is made—everything past that point is just reactionary.

For me, one of the hardest things to get clear on is what I'm good at because when I'm good at it, it comes really easy. So I think, "*Anybody can do this.*" But just because you find it easy doesn't mean somebody else does too. For example, there's a special skill in connecting with people and making them feel comfortable about sending you referrals.

The opposite is true as well. There are things you really don't like doing that other people love doing. So connect with them and let them do those things. Sometimes we feel guilty about having our staff do something we hate because we're transferring our feelings onto them. However, when you have the right team, it's like peanut butter and chocolate—the perfect match! While you are bringing in the business, someone else gets them to close.

Where Top Producers Focus

What most loan officers focus on are non-money-making activities—things like making promo materials (i.e., flyers and logos), having events but no follow-up, pipeline reports, trying to get a price exception, credit repair, chasing docs and conditions, putting out fires, running DU/LP, calling underwriters, etc... most of which are post-application activities.

Most LOs Work On:

- Promotion Material
  - Flyers/Logo
  - Promotion
  - Events no follow up
- Pipeline reports
- Price exceptions
- Rates
- Paperwork
- Problem Files
- Typically post application activities

Top Producers Focus On:

- Sales activity
- Agent meetings
- Giving presentations & scripting
- Sales Activity
- Coaching and Accountability
- Events with follow up
- Sales activity
- Conversion
- P&L – cost management
- Recruiting

What top-producing loan officers focus on are things like: **sales activity**, having appointments and meetings with real estate agent referral partners, giving presentations and scripting, **sales activity**, coaching and accountability, events with follow-up, conversions, **sales activity**, P & L or cost management, recruiting, **sales activity**. You'll notice that sales activity is there four times. That's because sales activity is their focus—not the fulfillment activity. That is a very important point.

Before I go further, consider this. Someone I really admire is a sales trainer named Brian Tracy. I'm a huge fan of him and his work. One of his famous books is *Eat That Frog!* It's a book about procrastination and one of the concepts in the book is if there's something you hate doing, just knock it out first thing and get it done. He gives an example of if you have to eat a frog every day at work, instead of sitting there and dreading it all day long, which will take up all your brain power, just walk in the office, grab that frog first thing at 9 a.m. and choke it down. Just eat it and be done with it.

I'm a huge fan of Brian, but when I first heard that idea, I did not like it at all. Why? Because I don't eat frogs anymore. The problem with eating a frog is, if you close more loans and have more frogs to eat, you're going to suppress your success because you don't want to eat frogs. So you'll keep your production on the lower side so you only have to do that activity you hate doing fewer times. Whereas if you eliminate the activity you hate doing, and only do the activity you love, then there's no frogs to eat. And you will grow your business because there's no bad effect from it.

The one thing I have found about "frog eating," is that my frogs are somebody else's filet. The stuff I hate doing is exactly what somebody else loves doing. And so my frogs are their filet and their frogs are my filet. Now I just outsource!

What should you outsource?

The things you're currently doing that drain you, the things you should be doing but you've been neglecting, whatever the "frogs" are in your mortgage business—you can delegate everything (and I do mean EVERYTHING!).

Now if you combine your Triad of Awesomeness Exercise (and identify what is A activity and B activity), the 80/20 principle AND you stop eating frogs, you can make a LOT more money! In fact, I'm going to show you in the next few pages how to make 160% more money.

How to Make 160% More

Let's start with the 80/20 Principle, which says that 20% of our effort makes 80% of our income. (Conversely, 80% of our effort is responsible for only 20% of our income.)

How to Make 60% More

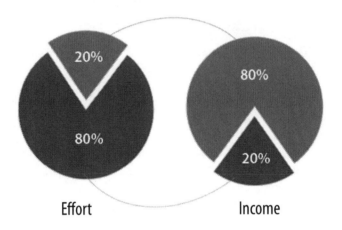

Effort   Income

Let's say, for the sake of round numbers, you are making $100,000 a year.

Applying our rule, 20% of your day (your effort) is making $80,000 of those dollars—and ALL the rest of the other activity added up, meaning 80% of your day—only gives you $20,000.

So if you can identify what that 20% activity actually is (Activity A) and do that exact same activity again (remember the "stacking" picture?), that would give you another $80,000. Now you're doing 40% effort and you're getting 160% result. Pretty cool, huh?

80% + 80% = 160%

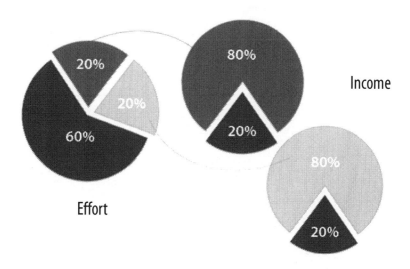

20% of an 8 hour day is roughly 1hr 45min. If I start my day at 9:00 a.m., I would be done with my first 20% by 10:45. If I add my second round, I could go home at 12:30, and still make 160% of my income because I'm doing the right activity. The key is doing the EXACT same activity again. Not a different one.

Here's a quick exercise that will help you identify what is YOUR Activity A and what is Activity B.

Below is a short list of what happens in the life of most loan officers every day:

- Check emails
- Recruit (if you're a branch manager)
- Return calls
- Talk to clients with files in progress
- Collect docs or chase conditions
- Put out fires
- Lock loans
- Keep in touch with past database
- Run DU/LP
- Get supplies
- Hire/Train Team
- Call leads
- Take applications—meet with clients
- Plan monthly mailer
- Execute monthly mailer
- Run errands
- Video marketing
- Bookkeeping / payroll
- Networking with other top LOs
- Plan Day
- Print flyers
- Teach classes at real estate offices
- Social media marketing
- Talk to underwriter
- Status updates
- Learn new loan programs
- Go to closings
- Call / meet with referral partners

Whew, no wonder you're tired at the end of the day—look at what you're choosing to do with your day!

Pretend you were only allowed to do one thing eight hours a day, five (whoops, make that four!) days a week, for the next two weeks. What is the one thing—and nothing else—that would have the largest impact on your business ninety days from now? Or, if you DON'T do it, it could put you out of business. Take a second and underline your choice.

You might choose teaching classes. What if I was kind and said you got to pick one more thing... maybe you'd pick calling and meeting referral partners? And what if I was super kind and said you got to pick one last thing... maybe you would choose taking applications and meeting with clients? So picture this—what would your business look like if for the next 30 days, all you did was those three activities: teaching classes at local real estate agent offices and/or the local Board of Realtors, or by using Zoom.com meetings, then following up with those agents through phone calls and face-to-face meetings or one-on-one video meetings, (resulting in them sending you referrals); and finally taking applications and working with those referrals? If that's all you did for the next 30 days and nothing else got in your way, what would your business look like 90 days from now?

Every time I've done this exercise with someone, they've answered, *"it would be amazing!"* And I have to agree.

Now I don't know what your three things are—I just picked three randomly—so your three things might be something different. But what are the three things that will have the most impact on your business? I guarantee it's not running errands. I guarantee it's not getting supplies. I guarantee it's not checking emails. And I guarantee it's not putting out fires or talking to the underwriter or even learning new loan programs. It's going to be something to do with selling.

Right now, write down the ONE THING you do that brings in the most money—the one, single activity.

Some people would say *"taking applications."* That's a good one, but something had to happen to bring that application into your business.

Some people would say *"go to closings, because I get to meet the agents in person."* But something had to happen for that closing to take place. You have to go to "the source of the Nile" to find the source of the application or closing.

For most loan officers, that one thing is going to be talking with referral partners or marketing to their past database.

Now that you've written that activity down, here's my next question… how many hours (or minutes), if any, did you do that specific activity last week? And preparing for the activity does not count—only count the actual "doing" of it.

The average answer I hear as I tour the country is usually "zero". No wonder we get "stuck" in our business and can't grow!

What if you could do your one activity for 8–10 hours a week? You would have amazing growth.

Say you are currently closing five loans a month doing two hours of focused activities per week… logically, to double your business, you would have to do four hours of the same activity. Sounds easy, right? But to do that, you'll have to take some activities off your plate.

If we look at our list again, the ones underlined are the ones that bring in the money; everything else is what keeps you from doing your number one activity.

- Check emails
- <u>Recruiting if you're a branch manager</u>
- Return calls
- Talk to clients with files in progress
- Collect docs or chase conditions
- Put out fires
- Lock loans
- <u>Keep in touch with database</u>
- Run DU/LP
- Getting supplies
- Post Office run
- <u>Calling leads</u>
- Take applications—meet with clients
- <u>Planning monthly mailer</u>
- Do monthly mailers
- Run errands
- Video marketing
- Bookkeeping / payroll
- <u>Networking with other top LOs</u>
- Plan Day
- Printing flyers
- <u>Teach classes at real estate offices</u>
- Social media marketing
- Talk to underwriter
- <u>Status updates</u>
- Learn new loan programs
- Go to closings
- <u>Calling / meeting referral partners</u>

The ones not underlined are the things you need to farm out and get some help on… let somebody else help do that while you go and bring in more loans. That's the secret sauce of top producers. That's what makes it all happen. Any time you spend doing an activity that an assistant can do, it robs you of income because you aren't selling.

In any business, it is the salesman who makes the money, not the customer service agent.

The Source of the Nile

Let's do something to start shifting your mindset. For the next week, as you're doing different activities, start asking yourself: is this the number one activity that makes me money AND is this the source of the Nile?

We've got to do that because to go from five loans a month to 20 loans a month isn't as easy as saying *"I'll just do four times as much as I am already doing."* There's not enough time in the day! You can't schlog through four times the leads, four times the applications, four times the conditions and fires, nor attend four times the closings!

Maybe you've been attending your closings. But if you had 20-30 of them to go to, when would you have time to sell? Now you might say, *"wait a minute, Carl—going to closings is a good activity. That's where I met Realtor Bob as the listing agent of that deal. Through him, I met Realtor Susan. Through Realtor Susan, I met Realtor Dan. And they're all sending me business today."*

That might be all fine and dandy. But if you're waiting until the closing to meet those listing agents, you're too late. If we're both working on a file for the same agent and you're waiting until closing to meet with the listing agent, I've already met with them. My team has already met with them. We meet them as soon as we get the contract in the door. We are proactive about our activity. We don't wait.

Getting crystal clear about what makes me money and what doesn't is the number one thing I did to explode my business. And it's worked for the thousands of loan officers I have privately coached as well.

Now I realize everything else has to get done—just not by me. Teamwork makes the dream work.

Celebrating Friends

That reminds me of a story about Suzanne, a dear friend of mine who lives down in south Florida. When I met her at one of my events, she was a single mother of four wonderful daughters, working nights and weekends and closing five to seven loans a month. If she took a vacation, she worked all the way through it.

She approached me during one of our breaks and said, *"Carl, if you could help me take a real vacation, you would change my life."* I said, *"You've never been on a vacation with your family?"* She said, *"Well, sort of… we'll go to Disney but I'll tell the girls to catch a ride while Mommy goes to make a phone call real quick. Or we'll be at the beach and the girls will want to play in the water. I'll tell them to go ahead and play—I'll catch up with them soon. I'm going to sit here and make a couple of phone calls. So yes, I go on vacation, but it always ends up with me working."*

We sat down and mapped out a plan (Activity A and B), who her first hire would be and the rest as they say, is history. Now she takes a vacation once a month. Some of those vacations are a four-day weekend, sometimes a week, sometimes it's a two-week trip to Europe. But every single month, she goes on vacation or just takes a week off and chills by her private pool. And, by the way, she closes a whole lot more loans now all while spending massive amounts of time with her daughters. She is a true role model that has inspired thousands of loan officers across the nation at this point.

In fact, as I am writing this, she is scheduled to close more than forty loans. So she's gone from five to seven loans a month to closing twenty, thirty, sometimes forty a month while going on a vacation or taking blocks of work days off every single month.

How would it change your life if you were closing 3-4 times your current volume AND taking a monthly vacation?

Need more proof? Here's another great win!

This is David H. from Pittsburgh on top of Mount Rainier. It's 5:45am on a Saturday morning. He sent me this picture and a note that says, *"here we are covering the Freedom Club in glory! I went with*

my top title company's owner, one of my top Realtors, took a week off, and rarely checked emails or voicemail. My team did a great job while I was away and found a couple of 'soft spots' in my process. Last year was my best year ever. I personally closed 315 units for $79.5 million. My total team closed 965 units for $215.4 million."

Yet he still has time to take the weekends and evenings off. That's what I want for you too.

And, by the way, he got to shore up his processes (those "soft spots") when he returned so things will run even smoother on his next vacation.

So who does the work when you're out of office? Your assistant(s) (AKA LOA's, LP's, or Junior LO's). We'll talk about that next.

Chapter 3

Your Assistant

So we talked about Activity A and Activity B. If you're going to be doing Activity A, which is the activity that brings in the business, you're going to need help.

In my private Facebook group, somebody asked the question, *"Hey, when you get an assistant, how many more closings should you get?"*

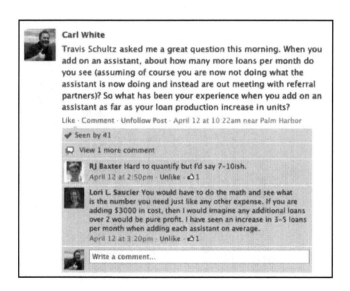

RJ, one of our leaders said, *"I'd say seven to 10."* And Lori said, *"three to five."* Myself, I find somewhere around 5–7, give or take.

Let's use our earlier math... if I'm making $2,000 per closing, and I bring in another 5–7 loans a month, that would be an extra $10,000–14,000 a month in revenue.

And let's say that assistant costs $3,000–$4,000 a month. If you could put $4,000 in a machine and $14,000 popped out, who would say no to that? That's the biggest no-brainer ever. Especially if they're doing everything you hate doing and you're working less hours—talk about a win-win.

I've heard a lot of LO's say, *"well, Carl, I can't afford an assistant right now, so what do I do?"* I'm here to tell you that you can't afford one because you ARE one. If you don't have somebody doing those B activities, it means you're the assistant and assistants can't afford assistants. So you have to figure out a way to make this happen.

I Can't Afford One Now

My first assistant worked four hours a day, one day a week. During those four hours, I put my war paint on and made a ton of phone calls to real estate agents. More on that in a minute.

The next thing I hear from loan officers is, *"wait a minute, Carl— my company won't pay for my assistant."* Well, guess what? Neither does mine! I pay for my assistants.

Here is the big question: What is the cost of NOT doing something? It's likely currently costing you $10–15,000 in lost revenue a month not to have help. It's costing you $15,000 a month—or more—to have more headaches!

The "How Can I Help You More?" Script

Here's how you can ask your Branch Manager to help you out with an assistant.

Go to them and say, *"<Manager Name>, I really enjoy working with you. I can't thank you enough. You're just a class act and you provide a great platform for getting our loans closed on time. It's going really great. I go home in the afternoon sometimes and think I'm so thankful for you and how can I help you even more. How can I show my gratitude? And I know what the answer is—it's to help you make more money. And <Name>, here's how I'm going to do that. If you could provide someone to help me, I could go out and get more sales. More sales lets me close more loans. And when I close more loans, you make more money. <Name>, would you help me make you more money?"*

Who would say no to that?

If you're just getting started, you might give yourself a quota. You might say, *"and <Name>, I tell you what… I'm asking you to trust me for the next 90–120 days. If you help pay for my assistant, while they're doing the B activity, here's the A activity I'm going to be doing."*

Then map out what you're going to be doing and how that will have you closing more loans.

You might also add, *"I'm closing five (or your number) loans per month now. And in 90 days, if I don't have that up to eight loans per month (or add 3–5 loans to your stated number) with this extra help, we can get rid of them and I'll never bother you about it again. I just need you to trust me for 90 days. Will you trust me for 90 days?"*

If they say no, there may be some deeper issues. Who wouldn't help you for 90 days if they knew it would help them make more money? Of course they would—unless you've given them reason in the past not to trust you. So of course they will.

Now, if you need help mapping all this out, reach out to us here at the Mortgage Marketing Animals. We'll get on the phone and we'll help you with it. Just click on the link in the footer of this book or in the bonus section of this book and schedule your call with us. (And there's no charge for this—we want to help you. We'll help you with the map-out, the scripting, laying out your calendar and the list of activities for you and your assistant.)

Another option if you're working for a larger company is to find one of the branch managers or another loan officer who already has an assistant and partner up with them for a period of time. They're probably going to get some of your basis points to help pay for the assistant. But again, do you want 100% of a grape or 50% of a watermelon?

You already know my first assistant only worked four hours per week. She came in every Wednesday morning and she'd do nothing but answer the phone and monitor my emails so I could make outbound phone calls that generated new referrals.

I'll never forget the first day she came in and freed up those four hours. I put my warpaint on, made four hours of phone calls and brought in two loans. That revenue allowed me to add an additional four hours, which brought in a couple of more loans which more than paid for her to start working full-time.

And that's how I started—four hours at a time! It's just when she was there, I hammered the phone calls and the meetings and it paid for itself—in fact, it more than paid for itself, and actually gave me another $10,000 or more in profit almost immediately. It's what got me my start. And then I got another assistant, and another assistant, until we made a team—and that team now helps me generate millions of dollars in revenue each year.

As we got busier, I found I didn't have enough time to get all my sales activities done consistently and so I added a position that has been a game changer for me. Meet Diane—I call her my Director of "Who".

My Director of "Who"

The Director of "Who"

The credit for this strategy goes out to my good pal Dean Jackson again. One of the biggest mistakes most loans officers (and, really, most entrepreneurs) make is they ask "How?" instead of "Who?"

I'll explain but, first, we need to back up a bit. Anytime a loan officer or branch manager tells me they want to close more loans, I always ask, "*Why?*" Most have the same "Why" I do and here it is... I want my kids to graduate from college (one is in medical school) so they have no student loan debt. I also want to make sure my wife and kids are taken care of in case something ever happens to me. I want to own all my properties debt-free, which I now do. And I want to take my family on a lot of vacations—we go to Europe for 3–4 weeks every year. We're also building a center for abused women in Colombia, South America and we support a local church and a couple of missionaries. These are my "WHYs."

Once you know your "Why," the next step is, "WHAT?" What do you need to do to make it happen? WHAT is your sales game plan. Let's say I'm going to set up Facebook marketing. That means creating copy, doing video marketing and online marketing.

So my "why" is to help my family and to bless other families. My "what" is to start doing Facebook marketing to increase my loan closings. Most loan officers / branch managers would make the mistake of asking, "How" do I do this Facebook marketing? Or "How" do I do video marketing, or "How" do I set up my CRM program, or "How" do I set up those tools we use to market to our past database? Asking "How" is the fatal flaw. Here's why...

When you look at the following diagram, on the left side you'll see timelines—that's the arrow with the notches on it. These timelines could be hours, days, weeks, months and, in my case, sometimes years trying to figure out "how" to do something. The WHY and WHAT might only take a few minutes to solve, but the HOW can take a long period of time. Once I know how, then I "DO" and I'm done.

My Director of "Who"

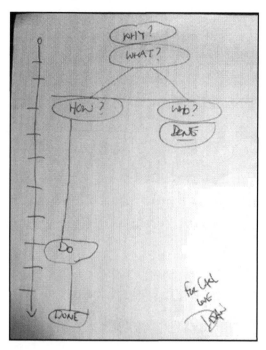

Dean shared a better way of doing it. We still ask "WHY". (For me, it was my family and other families.) We still ask "WHAT?" (meaning the tactic, like, Facebook advertising or video marketing.) However, I don't ask "HOW" anymore—I ask "WHO"... who else can do this? When you ask WHO, they already know HOW so there's no downtime trying to figure out HOW—they already know that answer. Now it's WHO? Then I'm done and onto the next WHAT. So don't ask HOW—ask WHO.

Because we have so many WHATs/HOWs going on, my Director of Who—Diane—keeps track of the WHOs. We have someone helping with Facebook marketing, someone helping with email marketing, someone helping with video marketing, someone helping write these books, someone managing my mortgage branch, someone recruiting loan officers to my team, someone managing my schedule, someone managing my sales team and someone managing my IT (plus a whole lot more). That's a lot of someone's.

So we don't ask HOW—we ask WHO and Diane keeps track of it all. And that's how I'm able to have a team who closes over $700 million worth of loans last year, on track to close over $1 billion this year, AND run one of the most successful loan officer training programs in the world today—all while working 32 hours per week. Because I ask WHO, not HOW. And that's what I want you to start doing too so you have greater freedom and better results too.

The Single Most Valuable Activity = Building Your Team

Here is the most valuable piece of information I think I could give you:

> *Building a team, managing that team and*
> *doing it profitably is likely the most valuable*
> *activity any business will ever do.*

Your team can literally do ANYTHING in your mortgage practice. If you have the right "Who," they can sell, manage, process, assist, put out fires, set appointments, manage relationships, structure your deals… anything! It may take time to get the team in place, but anything is possible.

One thing I've learned through the years is the team that got you to where you are now may not be the same team to take you to the next level. You'll need to learn to be ok with that. It's

What I Learned from the Punk Kid

The team that got you to where you are now may not be the same team to take you to the next level . . .

A word from the peanut gallery — "My number one take away at your last event was 'the team who got you where are now may not be the team that takes you to the next level.' I have a whole new team." (closing 25+ a month) —Pat Fitzgerald, San Antonio, TX.

a different skill set, a different level of people that can help at different stages of your business growth over time.

My first assistant, Jeanette, was amazing at helping me go from 3–4 loans a month to 10–12 loans a month. But then we kind of capped out there. I had to get someone else to help me get from 10 loans a month to 30 loans a month. And now the entire team closes somewhere between 450 to 700 plus loans each and every month (and no one is left from my original team).

A common question I get asked is, "*Carl, when should I get an assistant? When I have a certain amount of closings per month or when I'm too busy?*" My answer is a resounding "*NO!*"

You Must Invest Ahead

Would a NASCAR racer ever say, "*As soon as I win the Daytona 500, then I'm going to go get that fast engine*"? Or would an NFL owner ever say, "*As soon as we win the Super Bowl, then I'm going to go get that winning head coach or world-class quarterback*"? No!

You buy the fast engine, *then* you win the Daytona 500. You get the great coach or great quarterback, *then* you win the Super Bowl. You have to invest ahead. You have to have the help first and then you achieve greatness.

What Your Assistant Does

So what does your assistant do? Just about anything. Your assistant will answer your phone calls, handle your emails, manage your social media accounts, confirm your one-on-one appointments, make coffee, make your lunch, run your errands, handle all your mailings and set up events. On the loan side, they will put out the fires, collect the docs, call back your leads, run scenarios, take applications, run DU, sign disclosures and do income analysis. Everything you don't want to do—all your frogs—are what your assistant will handle. You come up with the strategic things—the ideas—and then somebody else works those ideas for you.

What Does Your Assistant Do?

- Answer all phone calls
- Check all your email
- Manage social media
- Confirm your one-on-one appointments
- Make lunch / make coffee
- Run errands
- All mailings
- Put out fires
- Collecting docs
- Put your leads on your computer every morning
- Everything you don't want to do … handle your frogs

When our team does the fulfillment side of things, it frees us up to do the sales activities (which is where the money is!). So what does this look like?

What You Do

Here is a sample list of "A activities" you should be focusing on to build your business..

What Do You Do?

- Teach classes at real estate offices
- Plan your marketing (not necessarily implementing it)
- Go to places agents hang out
- Call your leads
- Make presentations
- Mastermind with other like-minded people
- Strategic planning every 2 weeks
- Recruiting additional loan officers
- Only the things that you want to do

Teaching classes (whether in person or virtually) and then following up like a rockstar is an amazing way to meet and build relationships with agents. Building out a marketing plan that includes calls, texts, emails, social media, video marketing, advertising and face-to-face or one-on-one Zoom video conference meetings is another great use of your time. If you enjoy it, attending association meetings or other events where agents hang out is another way to grow your referral partner sphere. Of course, calling your leads and following up with clients are great money-making activities too.

One of my favorite activities is masterminding with other successful loan officers and learning new ideas I can implement in my business. And, as a successful, non-producing branch manager, recruiting talent in my branch has been wildly successful.

Let me ask you this: what is the single thing—the one single activity—that makes you most of your money? That's what you do. Everything else is farmed out to somebody else. This is strategy. Strategy reduces stress because you future-think potential issues and opportunities, then plan the right resources to achieve your business goals.

I can already hear you saying… *"but, Carl, I'm a control freak."* This is one of my personal favorite myths to bust so let's get on it.

Let's compare the "one-man band" with the conductor of The Boston Pops. Who makes the most money? The conductor does.

"But, I'm a control freak..."

Who has a private parking spot at the Coliseum? The conductor. Whose picture is on the album? Again, the conductor. Who gets all the fame? The conductor. Who gets invited to the Mayor's breakfast? The conductor. So, while the conductor gets the fame and fortune, the one-man band, well… honestly, he looks a bit like a clown.

When I first started in this amazing business, I thought everybody looked at me with awe and inspiration because I was doing everything; I was the "one-man band." I was doing literally everything in my mortgage business! And then in a moment of clarity, I thought, *"hmmm… wait a minute. The only people who are impressed by me looking like a clown are other "one-man bands."* High producers would roll their eyes behind my back and say, *"that Carl is doing everything. It's crazy. Who does that?"*

Please don't hear me calling you a clown. I am telling you what I discovered on my journey so it can help you somehow. It's not as impressive as we think it is to do everything ourselves. You will burn yourself out and you can't scale your business.

Two Shocking Facts

In my mortgage coaching business, we get loan officers who say, *"but Carl—my clients and referral partners NEED to talk to me about everything."*

News flash!!! No, they don't. Let me give you two shocking facts.

Shocking Facts #1 and #2

#1: We aren't nearly as important as we think we are

#2: They just want the money, and they want it on time

Shocking fact number one. We are not nearly as important as we think we are and, shocking fact number two, they don't care about ME—they just want their money. And they want it on time. They don't want the answer from ME—they just want the answer and they want it now.

If our referral partners MUST speak with us or have their clients speak with us, it is our own fault. We have taught them this behavior, or we have hired people who don't know what they are doing and have given our agents cause to feel this way.

Clients and referral partners don't want to talk to YOU specifically! They just want the results. They want the right answer. They want their money. They want their house. And they want it all stress-free! As long as you teach them that *"when you call my team, you're getting a faster, easier and better answer than when you talk to me,"* they're happy to talk with your team. They don't talk to you because you're the only one in the world who can do a mortgage. They talk to you because in the past, you've taught them it's the only way they close on time. Start teaching them something else.

Loan Officer Vending Machine

I've learned if real estate agents and borrowers could walk up to a vending machine, push a button and have their loan and commission checks pop out (without them having to talk to a soul), they would do it in a New York second. This means we simply need to teach customers that our team can totally take care of these activities.

How do you teach people to talk to your team? Let's get into that next.

Chapter 4

Scripting That Works

I have found that giving my team a script to follow makes all the difference in the world.

The Dr. Butler Script

One of the best scripts we've come to rely upon is what we call the "Dr. Butler" Script. My lovely bride's visit to our local dentist (and personal friend) inspired me to come up with this script.

While having dinner one night my wife said, *"Dr. Butler called today."*

"Really?," I asked.

"Yep, I went and had my teeth cleaned yesterday and he called today to see how I was doing. Wasn't that nice of him?"

"Did something go wrong during your appointment?," I asked.

"No, nothing went wrong. He just called to see how I was doing after my teeth cleaning," she answered.

I thought, *"how in the world did he have time to call 40–50 patients like this?"* I didn't see how he would have time.

Then I asked her, *"so you spoke to him personally?"*

She responded, *"well, no, it was Jill in his office but, while he was working, he called her to come over and asked her to please call me and see how I was doing and to let him know. Wasn't that nice of him?"*

"Hmmmm....very interesting," I thought, *"I need to learn more."*

So I called Dave (Dr. Butler) and I said, *"Hey Dave, who's Jill in your office?"*

He tells me Jill is his "secret weapon" and that she makes all his check-in calls with scripts he wrote which make the patient feel special and like it is him doing the calling. I asked him for the scripts and adapted them to my business. One secret is mentioning the "doctor's" name over and over, not the caller's name.

It went something like this, *"Dr. Butler asked me to call you and find out how you're doing. What should I tell him?'*

Here's the kicker—she doesn't even live in the same state. In fact, she lives in a small town in Alabama. His office just sends her a list of the previous day's clients. And she calls on his behalf. Other than a quick introduction and the beginning of the call, everything is about him. *"Dr. Butler wanted me to call you." "Dr. Butler wanted to know..." "Dr. Butler wanted me to tell you."*

You can use the same script, and others like it, for your clients and referral partners.

The Script that Works

- Dr. Butler story…
- "Carl wanted me to call you to tell you…" (never do they say "I", always "Carl wanted you to know…")
- Chrissy is my partner, she specialized in this and will help you with the application process.
- You upsell your team to the people you work with, your team upsells you.

Following are some scripts your assistants could use for your borrowers.

— *LO Carl wanted to move you to the front of the line and get you started right away. I'm going to get some information from you and set up a time for your consultation with him.*

— *LO Carl wanted me to let you know we need a little more information. He wanted to know if you could send us these items within 24 hours so we can keep on schedule?*

— *LO Carl wanted me to call you right away and let you know that you are CLEAR TO CLOSE! Congratulations. He got tied up with a client but wanted to get you the good news right away!*

— *LO Carl wanted me to ask you if there were any friends, family members or co-workers that you knew who might need some help with a mortgage? No? That's ok. Can he ask you a favor? (Yes). If you hear of someone, can he count on you to send them over to him? He would like to help your family and friends also, so can he count on you for that?*

— *LO Carl asked me to call and see if you guys were looking at houses this weekend or if you were taking a break and doing something different. (Respond appropriately) OK. Well, he just wanted me to remind you to call us first thing Monday morning when you find your house! We've got our fingers crossed over here and hope this is your weekend! We are looking forward to getting you into the home of your dreams. By the way, if you come across anyone else looking to buy a home, can Carl count on you to give him a call?*

Here are some great scripts your team can use for your referral partners.

— *LO Carl asked me to call you and let you know that the Smith file is right on schedule. He said he loves working with you and your team. In fact, he told me if there was a magic button he could push and only work with agents like you, he would push that button all day every day! Is there anyone else you are working with we can help? We would love to see you at the closing table twice this month.*

— *LO Carl asked me to call you and find out if you had any time available to meet this week. He is so excited to be working with you and makes it a point to meet with the agents he is in transaction with to explain our processes. Do you have 15 minutes or so this week when he can treat you to a coffee and go over a few things?*

— *LO Carl asked me to call you and let you know we are waiting on some items from the borrower. They have exceeded their 24–hour deadline for returning documentation. I just wanted to give you a heads-up and let you know if we don't hear back from them soon, we might have to delay closing. He asked me to let you know we've called, texted and emailed and still haven't heard back. He just didn't want it to come as a surprise if we had to delay because he considers you a friend as well as a partner.*

Can you see how using scripts like these could be a gamechanger? It's as if YOU actually made the call yourself, but you didn't. Now you are free to do some "Activity A" and bring in more deals. That's how to get over the "Loan Officer Rollercoaster."

The key to all this is upselling your team. It's important you tell everyone that your team is amazing. And if you don't have an amazing team, get one right now! If you need help with the hiring process, reach out to us and give us a call at (727) 787-2275, text us at (727) 240-3064 or email us at **Support@TheMarketingAnimals.com**.

The Radar Script

Here is a great script to use on referral partners to have them calling your team instead of calling you for everything. For instance, when you meet with a real estate agent, have this conversation.

> *"My favorite thing about working with seasoned real estate agents is that they understand the Superbowl team concept. They know the quarterback can't win the game all by him(her)self—it takes a TEAM—a village—to get a family into a home. I've hired some amazing unicorns back in my office so that your clients always get a VIP-front of the line pass. My team of specialists really know their stuff. In fact, we call my loan partner and mortgage guru "Radar." She has this uncanny knack for identifying issues before they ever come up. It's absolutely incredible. So anytime you have a lead for me, she's going to move your client to the front of the line and help them get started. Is that something you think will help you?"*

Nobody's going to say, *"No—move me to the back of the line."*

In my office, we don't even have a voicemail system. One of my assistants answers the phone or, if it's after hours, it goes to our answering service. They answer just like the receptionist in my office would and take a message. They relay the message to us via email and text and let the caller know we will reach out within 15 minutes if it is during office hours or first thing in the morning if it is after hours. When you call my number 24/7, someone is always going to answer the phone.

You might be thinking this hand-off might be difficult, especially with long-time referral partners. I suggest forwarding your cell phone to the office so you don't even receive the calls. When your staff answers the phone, they can use a script something like this:

> *"It's a great day at Carl's Mortgage Company, how can I help you? You need a mortgage? And who may we thank for referring you our way? Realtor Mary? WOW! We love her! Have you bought a lotto ticket this week? You should! You hit the jackpot when you got her! Let me grab Carl for you! Whoops, looks like he just picked up the other line. Since you work with Mary, let's move you to the front of the line. Let me gather a little info from you and set up a consultation with Carl so that you aren't playing phone tag. Would you prefer to give me the information over the phone or would you prefer to take advantage of our secure online application from the comfort of your own home? Great! So that Carl can be prepared for your time together, could you send over your last couple of pay stubs and bank statements as well? That will help him have a complete picture of what you are trying to accomplish. If you can get that over to us right away, I can set up your consultation with him at 4pm this afternoon. Does that work for you?"*

Now I don't think it is necessary to explain to your referral partner(s) what you are doing, but if you feel you must, here is a great way to do it.

"Hey Agent Mary, I just want to tell you how much I appreciate you. Because of the referrals you've given to me, you've helped me put my son and daughter through college. Now my boy is working with the Air Force as an electrical engineer helping our troops. And my little girl is in her final year of medical school and learning to save lives. So thank you! You know, I was talking with my wife last night and wondering what I could do to help make your life easier. Here's what we came up with. I want to move you and your clients into my VIP program. No one is ever going to hit my voicemail. My team will assist your clients immediately and set up a time for me to consult with your client so there isn't any phone tagging taking place. We will follow-up with them like green on a pickle and keep you informed as to where they are in the loan process. My team is going to become your team and we are going to build you up and resell you back to your client so that you get even more referrals from them. I can't wait to get you guys started with this and moving you and your clients to the front of the line!"

Nobody's going to tell you, *"no, move me to the back of the line. I don't want the extra help. I want to be at the back of the line. I'm going to leave a voicemail and play phone tag, Carl."*

Using this script, they aren't hearing, *"I'm too busy; I don't have time for you and your clients so talk to my assistant."* They hear, *"You're important. You matter to me. You're a VIP. Your time is valuable."*

> **HUGE NEWS FLASH:** Your staff needs to live up to the expectations you have set! They have to be A-class players. If you don't have A-class players on your team, get the first one and grow the team from there.

These scripts were responsible for helping me grow from a team of two to a team of over 100. I'm sure they will help you too!

The 10,000 Questions Problem-Solving Formula

Now that your referral partners and clients are working with your team, how do you empower your "unicorns" and keep them from asking you 10,000 questions? (If you have to answer every question, you are now the bottleneck in your business and will have problems growing and scaling.)

First, hire resourceful people. They're phenomenal at figuring things out—in our case, usually much better than I am. If they do need to ask a question, here is a little formula they go through to make sure they are ready to ask a solid question.

Problem Solving Formula

- Here's the situation
- Here's what I have done
- Here's the results of what I did
- Here's my question
- Here's what I think we should do

Before they ask a question, they have to work through what they can do on their own. *"Carl, here's a situation. Here's what I did, and here's the results of what I did. Now, here's my question but here's what I think we should do."*

How many questions do you think I get these days? That's right—almost none. That's because this formula requires they actually DO something before they ask a question.

I have found people ask me questions because a) I've made it easy for them (I'm Google), b) they're afraid they're going to make a mistake and disappoint me, or c) they're lazy.

First, I'm not Google anymore. I can't grow and scale a business if I am always answering questions. There are lots of resources available to help them find their answers. I'll make a list of those resources for them. (Someone else in the company, a favorite rep, a scenario desk, a processor or underwriter, a guideline manual, etc.)

Second, mistakes happen. As long as we learn from them and change our systems and processes so it doesn't happen again, there won't be a problem. Now if they make the same mistake two or three times, we've got a problem.

It's about empowering your team to act without fear and educate as you go in case something goes sideways. Remember, we're looking to free you up so you can focus on bringing new business in. If you're back in the office micromanaging stuff, it's not going to work out.

Third, if you have someone who is lazy and unresourceful, get rid of them. They aren't a unicorn and you don't work with lazy people.

A great way to rate your team is to give them a score from 1–10 where a seven is not an option. Those that grade as an eight or higher, they are a good long-term match for you. Those that grade less than six, well, it's time to replace them. Feed your stallions and get rid of the ponies. You need the best to be the best!

I love this little tent that sits on my desk. Facing them as they walk in, it says, *"what do you think we should do?"* I jump right to Question 5. If they say *"I don't know,"* I remind them, *"You don't have to KNOW what to do, I want to know what you **think** we should do."*

On my side of that little sign, it asks, *"Is this a good use of my time?"* It's an excellent reminder to use my precious time wisely. (Keep in mind I am not asking if the person is a good use of my time, I am asking if the situation is a good use of my time.)

Chapter 5

Excellent Help Requires the Right Mindset

Now let's chat about where we can find our unicorns. This could be a whole book by itself so I'll just highlight how we do it.

First, make the decision that you are looking for a UNICORN! This is someone who has the experience you are looking for and they have an amazing attitude.

A fact of nature is, 1% of employees are "superior", 4% are "excellent", 25% are "good", 60% are "fair", and 10% are "poor".

Which Employee Costs You Most In Lost Opportunities?

- Superior—1%
- Excellent—4%
- Good—25%
- Fair—60%
- Poor—10%

Most people answer "the poor employee". In actuality, it's the good employee that costs you most. We easily identify the "poor" ones right away and get rid of them.

Good employees are just average. And with average input, you get average results. Don't be average. We're looking for unicorns!

The best piece of advice I've ever received about hiring came from my good friend, Perry Belcher. He said, *"we hire people who tell us what to do, not the other way around."* He followed up with, *"and we're hiring."* I love that.

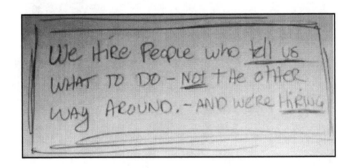

If I'm busy telling my team what to do, I'm NOT out getting new business. So I'm looking for people who would tell me, *"hey, Carl, you need to get out of the office and go do what you do. We got this."*

Now that you are committed to finding good talent, let's talk about the steps to make it happen.

Using Technology to Recruit Your Best Help

I would say our primary sources for recruiting talent are WizeHire.com, Indeed.com, and our own Facebook newsfeed.

WizeHire helps us place the ads, collect resumes, run DISC profiles, ask qualifying questions and rate candidates.

The DISC

We use a personality questionnaire to screen our applicants to see if they have the qualities we are looking for in our mortgage business. Anyone can take the test free of charge by going to **DiscProfileLink.com**. There are two assessments available there—one for a salesman (loan officer) and one for our support staff.

There are three sections of the profile. While I'll give you some general guidelines to look for, this subject could be a whole book by itself.

The DISC section tells you what a person's outward (observable) behaviors are to help categorize their probable responses in various situations. In respective order, this assessment measures Dominance, Influence, Steadiness, and Conscientiousness. If you are looking for a loan partner or loan assistant, you are looking for a low D, a mid to high I, a higher S and a mid to high C. If you are looking for a processor, you would want the C to be on the higher side. We look for high D, high I, lower S and lower C in a true salesperson (loan officer).

The Values section just tells you about someone's motivational drivers. There is no wrong answer here as this simply helps you know what makes them tick.

- Aesthetic—a drive for balance, harmony and form.
- Economic—a drive for economic or practical returns.
- Individualistic—a drive to stand out as independent/unique.
- Political—a drive to be in control or have influence.
- Altruist—a drive to help others altruistically.
- Regulatory—a drive to establish order, routine, and structure.
- Theoretical—a drive for knowledge, learning, and understanding.

The third section of the profile is about the candidate's Attributes to give you an idea of where their talents lie and how they think.

We don't hire someone unless they have taken this three-part assessment. While nothing is foolproof, we have found this gives us our best shot at finding what we are looking for; I highly recommend you require it as part of your hiring process too.

There will be times when, even though you do everything right (great interview, resume, experience and DISC), your new hire will not be a good match. In that case, remember to be quick in letting them go so they can find their next best career move and you can find the right person to get you what you need.

Where to Find Assistants

- Title companies
- Other mortgage companies
- Real estate offices
- Facebook/Indeed
- Tall of your friends you are looking for someone
- Real estate agents on your Monday Morning calls
- Zip Recruiter

We have found assistants at title companies, other mortgage companies, and real estate offices. We've also placed ads on Facebook and used hiring companies like Wize Hire or Indeed.com.

You can also ask your current employees to refer people they know or have worked with in the past—that's worked well for us. Your referral partners can keep an eye out for you, too. If they have worked with someone in the past they really enjoyed, ask them to give you their name.

The Egg Company Set Me Free

Not everyone is going to be a match for my team. You already know that the team who helped me get to one level of business usually did not have the skill level to take me to the next level. They were excellent (even unicorn-ish) at helping me get started, but struggled when we grew. In that case, I had decisions to make.

First, I have to determine if the struggle is simply too much volume or if it's lack of ability. If volume is the issue, I add to the team. If ability is the issue, I need to set them free to go help someone else get started.

Here's a quick story that helped me when I was struggling to let someone go.

Many moons ago, I washed eggs for a living. I worked for a big egg company in a little rural town called Zephyrhills. I thought I was going to work there forever. I was there for about 3–4 years, from 11th grade until two years after high school. I thought I was really good at my job. But one day I got fired.

I won't go into details, but let's just say when you put 21- or 22-year old Carl together with 750,000 eggs being washed a day, there's going to be some mischief. I pulled a prank on someone—actually, it was my boss—and I thought he would think it was funny. Well, he didn't—and he fired me. I was absolutely devastated.

That termination pushed me to join the Air Force, which led me to sitting around a campfire in Virginia one night where I had an epiphany. This epiphany brought me home to Florida, where I enrolled in college, met my lovely bride, and began my medical career. Eventually, I met my friend Ralph who got me into the mortgage business and the rest, as they say, is history!

Not too long ago, I happened to drive past the egg factory and decided to drop by and do a little reminiscing.

I wandered around for a bit and then I heard somebody yell out, "*Carl?!?*" I looked around and an old buddy of mine (I'll call him Rick) came up to me.

To say I was shocked would be an understatement. He looked

really worn and tired and like he had lived a hard life. Here he was some 30 years later, still washing eggs for somewhere around minimum wage, just like I was back so many years ago.

Now I'm not making judgment about my brother. My point is had I NOT been fired, I might still be working there too, still making minimum wage! I suddenly became very grateful I had been fired. It led me to where I am today.

Since then, I've met with tens of thousands of loan officers across the country and helped so many, and so many have helped me. And I've lived an epic life making millions of dollars in the mortgage business every year. None of that would have happened had my boss not fired me that day.

And so, I learned a very valuable lesson that has carried over into my mortgage business today. If someone isn't working out, I need to let them go. Chances are if I'm not happy as their "boss", it's likely they're not happy either. And what if, by holding them back, I keep them from finding their dream career, like I found mine?

While I was "good" at washing eggs, I'm in the 1% "Superior" group in the mortgage business—both as a non-producing branch manager AND as a successful mentor and coach. I've made tens of millions of dollars over the years by coaching other loan officers and by helping families buy houses. And I would have never discovered my talent had my "egg boss" not released me to go on my journey of awesomeness.

So, if you've got someone that's isn't a solid "8" out of 10, let them go because you may be holding them back from their epic story.

Now, don't get me wrong—I was devastated when I was fired. I was devastated and thought, *"oh, it can't get any worse than this."* But it was the one of the best things that ever happened to me. That put in motion a chain of events to a story I couldn't have written more perfectly for myself.

I beg you—don't put up with mediocrity! There are people out there who are a perfect match for you and your business.

Chapter 6

The Axe of Freedom

Ok—your real estate partners are on board, you have the right staff in place, and you are ready to roll. The next step is figuring out what to take off your plate so you can go out and do what you do best—BRING IN THE BUSINESS!

We do a very valuable exercise that we call the "Axe Of Freedom".

Axe of Freedom

First, write down a list of all those things you're doing in your mortgage office as a loan officer, branch manager or owner. I've got a partial list here to help get you started.

Loan/Office Stuff	Get purchase contract / addendums
Answer phones	Handwritten thank-you's
Attend closings	Homes for Heroes marketing
Bookkeeping	Initial intro call / email — Just ask
Call "preapproved-looking" buyers	Just Ask campaign
Call leads	Loan comparison software
Call realtors and referral sources	Lock loan
Chase conditions	Market to database (call and monthly mailer)
Check email	Meet with clients to sign 1003
Check voicemail	Office management
Check the website for leads	Quote rates
Collect initial docs	Recruiting
Collect / clear conditions	Refer to credit repair
Compliance stuff	Request disclosures
Coordinate closings	Research loans
Coordinate clear to close	Return calls
Create paper file	Review the closing documents
Deliver good and bad news	Review HUD
Denials	Review income / assets
Email broadcasts	Review underwriter conditions
Email needs lists	Review / print rate sheets
Email overnight 1003 package	Run DU or LP
Enter into your CRM	Run errands
Face-to-face meeting with referral partners	Scan packages

Send congratulation letters to all parties / Starbucks card	Thor's Hammer
	Update your CRM
Send a prequalification letter / video	Update loan board
Send text messages	Upload 1003 / Review fill-in
Sign disclosures	Write LOXs
Structure loan	
Submit loan to processor	**Marketing/Conversion Stuff**
Submit loan to underwriter	AMM invites — email and F/U calls
Take the initial application	Design Monthly Client Mailer
Talk to the underwriter	Facebook ads

Answer phones. Attend closings. Bookkeeping. Call "preapproved-looking" buyers. Call leads. Call realtors and referral sources. Chase conditions. Check email. Check voicemail. Check the website for leads. Collect initial docs. Collect / clear conditions. Compliance stuff. Coordinate closings. Coordinate clear to close. Deliver good and bad news. Denials. Email broadcasts. Email needs lists. Email overnight 1003 package. Enter into your CRM. Face-to-face meeting with referral partners. Get purchase contract / addendums. Handwritten thank you's. (Maybe) Homes for Heroes marketing. Initial intro call / email. Updates every Tuesday, (which is the Just Ask Program). Loan comparison software like Mortgage Coach or MBS Highway. Lock the loan. Market to database. Phone calls and monthly mailers. Meet with clients. Office management. Quote rates. Recruit, (if you're a branch manager). Refer to credit repair, if you do that. Request disclosures. Research loans. Return calls. Review the closing documents. Review income assets. Review underwriter conditions.

Run DU or LP. Run errands. Scan packages, (if you still do that). Send congratulation letters to all parties. Send a prequalification letter and or video. Send text messages. Sign disclosures. Structure the loan. Submit the loan to the processor. Submit the loan to the underwriter. Take the initial application. Talk to the underwriter. Thor's Hammer—(we're going to go over that). Update your CRM. And the list goes on.

As you can see, there are a lot of different things you do here.

Now, list all the employees (or job roles) in your office and go down the list and start assigning that job to someone on the team. Only assign each duty to one person (or job role if you have multiples). Here's an example of how one of my clients, Ken P., did it.

Ken is now a leader in our coaching organization, The Freedom Club, and is no longer doing "everything." But, this is what Ken sent me when he first joined The Freedom Club.

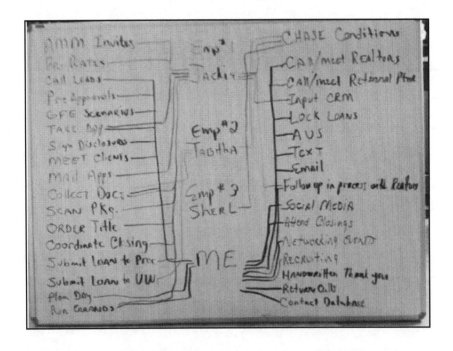

Even before you look at the details, what's the one glaringly obvious thing about the way things were set up in Ken's office? Yep, all roads lead to Ken. When I first saw this, I said, *"dear Lord, Ken, who wants to be the "me" in here, the Ken? Dude, I want to be Sheryl. Sheryl's only doing one job. That's the position I want to apply for!"*

Ken didn't even realize he was doing everything until he saw this—and his business looks drastically different today because of the changes he has made after working with my team. Ken is a super smart guy but, like many of us, couldn't see the forest for the trees on his own.

There are several ways you can do this exercise. You can do it like Ken did and put your names in the center of the list and draw lines to the jobs. You can write everyone's names in columns and list the jobs below them (see diagram below). You can copy the list above in Excel and then color code each job (Red—processor, Green—Loan Officer, Blue—Loan Partner, Orange—Receptionist, etc.)

If you are currently the one-man band, here is what I suggest. On a sheet of paper (or in your computer) make two columns. One is for you. The other one will be labeled, "New Hire." Go through the list and transfer everything that doesn't make you money or that you HATE doing. You now have the perfect job description for your new hire. If you need help with this, I have someone in my office who can lend a hand to help you out with this, no charge. Just give us a call at 727-787-2275 and set up a complimentary strategy session.

This is my favorite way of doing this exercise. You get complete clarity. And, like Josh, I recommend you put this up on a white-

Josh

Meet Realtors
Deligate Tasks
Just Ask Campaign
Answer Guideline Q's
Realtor Presentation

Sonny

• Answer Phones
• Answer Emails
• Take Apps
• Start Files
• Send Needs Lists
• Follow up w/ Clients
• Follow ups w/ Realtors
• Follow up calls w/ Insurance Agents
• Update MPC
• Follow ups w/ Jeremy
• Follow ups w/ Title Agents
• Request VOE's from WPB Office
• Send Disclosures
• Call Clients when they don't send docs
• Explain how to receive Disclosures to Clients
• Input Docs into Files
• Check what docs need updates for Sub.
• Submit Files to Jeremy
• Explain to Clients & Realtors what Mile-stone the File is at
• Explain what conditions need to be met when conditionally Approved
• Complete File Checklists
• Pull Credit if Client has Subpar Credit Explain their options to them
• Lock Rates
• Price Loans
• Update Josh's Calender

Francesca

• Call for meetings
• Set Appointments
• Confirm Appointments
• Handwritten Notes
• Call & Text past Database
• Call & Text pre-Approvals for check in
• Thor's Hammer
• End of Month Mailers
• Write on the white board - mama

Carla

• Putting out Fires
• Structuring Loans
• Selling Loans
• Run DU/LP
• Take Applications
• Check Email
• Lock Loans
• Send E Disclosures
• Go over Checklists
• Pre Approve Files
• Price Loans
• Review CD Before Closing
• Review LE
• Go over CD
• Return Calls
• Discuss Loans with Realt
• Monthly Mailer

board in your office where your employees, your partners and teammates can see it. (It lets everyone know that you're organized!)

A side benefit is we know how to fill in for each other if someone is on vacation, is out sick or if they begin another "journey of awesomeness" elsewhere :) AND you never hear, "oh, I thought you were going to do that. Or, I thought she was going to do..." This gives you complete clarity of who's doing what.

This gives you the ability to hold the team accountable and to find out where there are holes in your systems and processes and fix them. As you can see, it's a very, very, very, very powerful activity to do.

This exercise also gives you the ability to post job ads that are laser focused and that attract the right candidates. Simply list the items that the new hire will be doing, as identified by your Axe Of Freedom, and put those items as the job description. Complete clarity has been achieved relating to what you are looking for in your new hire. There is someone out there who will LOVE doing that job!

> **Hot Tip:** Use the DISC profile system (**DiscProfileLink.com**) to make sure your new hire's personality matches the job duties.

The Billionaire's Way

This short story proves my point. Not too long ago, I met with Kevin O'Leary, Mr. Wonderful from *Shark Tank*. I was allotted a few minutes to ask him a couple of questions. Talk about pressure! What do you ask a BILLIONAIRE???? Here's what I came up with. Sometimes the most obvious questions are best; *"Kevin, how do you make $1 billion? How do you become a billionaire?"*

And what he told me was simple but remarkable and it confirmed what I had been preaching! He said, *"Carl, you make a list*

of all those things that you're doing and find a replacement who could do some of those activities for you. With your freed-up time, go make more sales. Put some of those profits in your pocket and then use some of those profits to hire someone else to take more activities off your plate." Sound familiar?

Message from a Billionaire...

Make a list of all the things you do and find a replacement(s) that can do those activities for you.

Do that by making some sales, then hire somebody to take some off your list.

The make more sales with your new found "Free Time" and hire somebody else to take even more off your list.

Rinse and Repeat...

Some people are fearful of hiring people because they think, *"What if things slow up? I don't want to have to fire someone."*

Here are my thoughts on that. When I hire people, I'm offering opportunities. I'm offering an opportunity to work in an amazing place, for an amazing group of people and to help bring in more business for us, all while making themselves more valuable so that they get ever increasing financial rewards for doing so.

The way they bring in business is two-fold. First, they take things off my plate that allow me to go bring in more business. Second, when they have conversations with prospects and referral partners, they, they end their call asking for business on my behalf.

So, if we aren't growing, someone didn't do their job (and I know it wasn't me.) It's not my responsibility to make sure that they keep their job. It's my responsibility to give them an opportunity for them to run with it. It takes all the stress off of me.

Now you can give people the opportunity to work for you, knowing it's not your obligation to make sure they have continued employment—that's their job to do that. Take that stress off of you. Put them in charge of that.

Upgrading Your Activities

Remember this?

The activity that takes you from 0 loans to 4 loans / month may not be the same activity that will take you to 10 loans / month

The activity that takes you from 4 loans to 10 loans / month may not be the same activity that will take you to 30 loans / month

The activity that takes you from 10 loans to 30 loans / month is for sure not the same activity that will take you to 120 loans / month

Don't forget that the activity which takes you from 4 to 10 loans a month may not be the same activity that will take you to 30 loans a month. And the activity that takes you from 10 loans to 30 loans a month is—for sure—not the same activity that will take you to 120 loans a month, or 250 loans a month, or even 500 loans a month.

How do I know this? Because that's what we did this past spring/summer. And the activity that I'm doing as my team closes 700+ loans a month is certainly not the same activity I did when I was closing 4 loans a month.

Your activities MUST change! When I was doing four loans a month, going to closings was a good thing to do. Now there's no way in heck I could go to all those closings. And guess what? The more I refine my activities, the less time I work and the more $$$ per hour I make!

Guess What Top Producers Do...

- Chase conditions?
- Go to closings?
- Work "after hours"?
- Work weekends?

One thing I've noticed is some top producers chase conditions, some don't. Some top producers go to closings, some don't. Some top producers work after hours, some don't. Some work weekends, some don't. This started another great conversation in my head.

"So if I'm a top producer, I can chase conditions, go to closings, work after hours, and work weekends. OR, I can NOT chase conditions, go to closings, work after hours, or work weekends." My next thought was revolutionary! *"I'll take the NOT!"*

And I hope you choose to do the same in your business. It's good for you. It's good for your family.

Of all the A activities—consulting with clients, building real referral partner relationships, marketing, teaching classes or hiring talent—talent acquisition would top the list for me.

Why? Because when I bring on top talent, I can delegate all my lower income-producing activities to them. When I do that, I can focus on those very few things that give me my best and biggest results.

Chapter 7

Always Wear Black Pants

One of the promises I made early on in this book was to tell you why I always wear black pants.

I heard this a long time ago and have never forgotten it. Do you know the difference between fear and courage?

Fear is peeing in your pants. Courage is doing what needs to be done with wet pants on. Everyone experiences fear! I experience fear when I do stuff—it never goes away. It's just that people who succeed—the people who bring awesomeness to the world—they feel the fear and do stuff anyway. They wet their pants, so to speak, and then they do what they need to do with wet pants on.

So I jokingly say, *"that's why I always wear black pants."* This principle is life-changing.

I feel fear every time I go on stage. Yet I talk to thousands and thousands of people every year. I'm afraid every single time—I just put my big boy (black) pants on and do it anyway.

And when you push through that fear and do it anyway,

wonderful things will happen. So don't wait until you don't feel the fear. *'As soon as I feel confident enough, then I'm going to do it.'* Screw that! Take a page from Nike—Just Do It.

So as you read the principles and directions in this book, then decide how to apply them, well, just put your black pants on.

This Is A Perverted Industry

Another promise I made early on in this book was to talk about how we work in a perverted industry. (Stay with me here, it's not what you're thinking.) :=)

There aren't too many industries where both sales and fulfillment are handled by the same person. We talked about the one-man band but let's explore this further.

What if you walked into a Mercedes dealership and said, *"I need to talk to a salesperson about buying a new car today."* And the receptionist behind the desk said, *"I'm sorry. All the salespeople are in the back helping in the service department. But if you leave your name and your phone number, when they're finished doing that, they'll call you back."*

You would walk out of there thinking, *"what the heck is wrong with these people? I'm here trying to buy a new car and they've got salespeople changing tires? And ignoring people on the front lot?"* But that's exactly what's happening when we're chasing conditions. It's exactly what's happening when we're doing that "B" activity.

At car dealerships, there is one person who sells the car, one person who details the car, one person who fixes the car, and one person who does the financing (plus a whole lot more).

When you go to a fine restaurant, there is one person who seats you, another person who takes your order, another person who delivers the food, and yet another person who offers you the dessert menu. Someone different cleans the table. And someone else washes the dishes. There's someone who cooks and someone who makes drinks. There's also someone who manages it all!

It's only the mortgage business where the loan officer is expected to generate the lead, take the application, chase the conditions, AND close the loan. That's crazy—just absolutely crazy.

The only other industry I can think of where sales and fulfillment are handled by the same person is a hot dog stand. Generally, the stand owner shops for the food, drives the cart to its sales location and sets the cart up. Then, they cook the dog, sell the dog and wash the dishes/clean up when they're done. Don't be a hot dog stand owner—be the owner of a fine respectable company.

Picture this. You go to your doctor for a check-up and, in the reception area, he/she opens the little window and asks, *'Hey, can I help you?"* And you say, *"Uh yeah, I'm here to see you."* *"Perfect. Please fill out this insurance information, let me get your co-pay and get you into our database. Then I'm going to take you back and check your temperature, your blood pressure, and your weight, then I'll come in and diagnose you."*

You would think, *"what the heck is wrong with this doctor?"* You would think they must not be very successful if they're doing everything.

This just confirms we are in one of the weirdest industries ever where the loan officer is expected to do sales and fulfillment too. Don't do that anymore.

Curly from *City Slickers*

If you're old enough to remember that great movie *City Slickers* with Billy Crystal, Curly, the crusty cowboy, had a great line. He said," *the secret in life is one thing.*" I'm here to tell you the secret in the mortgage industry is "one thing." What is that one thing you do? What is that single activity that makes you most of your money? Do THAT and let other people do the rest of it. It's not about doing 10,000 different things, it's about doing one great thing, and then leveraging that.

Chapter 8

The Perfect Loan Process

Now that our foundation is laid, I'd like to show you how I get the maximum amount of stuff done in the least amount of time. I'm going to talk a little bit about what I call the Perfect Loan Process. This may be different than what you might have seen before. This process is going to walk you through how you do more of the A activities to bring in the loans and less of the B activities, the reactive stuff.

Let's say the phone rings and a receptionist answers it. Now this receptionist may be a loan officer assistant, a loan partner or a true receptionist—whoever it is, it is NOT you!

By the way, with web-based internet phone systems, this person doesn't even need to be in your office. There are several cloud-based systems like RingCentral, Grasshopper or 8 x 8. It doesn't matter which one you use. I just strongly recommend these types of phone systems. All of them allow you to use local numbers so it looks like outbound calls are coming from your office. We

The Phone Rings / Receptionist Answers It

Loan in Process   New Application

Loan Partner / Jackie

require everyone who works for us to use OUR system so no one slips through the cracks and so we maintain our database.

Normally when the phone rings, the caller asks for you. We always use what we call the "front of the line" script. Your receptionist will ask, *"is this about a loan in process or is this about a new mortgage?"*

If it's a loan in process, they say, *"hold on a sec, let me grab him/her. Whoops, looks like they just picked up the other line. Let me move you to the front of the line and speak with (insert name) who is very familiar with your file and can help you right away."* Then they transfer them to the loan partner or processor who is working on the file.

If it's a new application, it's a similar script. *"Hold on let me grab him/her real quick. Whoops, it looks like they just picked up the phone to help another family. Who did you say your Real Estate Agent/Realtor was? Mary? Oh, we LOVE Mary! Let's do this! I don't want you to have to wait. We try to give Mary's clients a VIP pass when we can. So, let's move you to the front of the line. Let me grab some information from you really quick and then let me make an appointment with (LO Name) so you aren't playing phone tag. There are a couple of ways we can get this info. I can take it from you now over the phone, or I can direct you to our very secure online application where you can fill it out. Which would you prefer?"*

If a loan partner answers that call, they could respond, *"(LO Name) is in a meeting. I can help you right now. I'm one of (LO Name)'s pre-approval specialists. We'll go ahead and start the application process just to move you to the front of the line. And then after I take that information, I'll set you up an appointment to talk to (LO Name). He/she'll talk about the different loan programs you qualify for, including perhaps some government programs you might be entitled to and wouldn't even know to ask about. So here, let's go ahead and get started."* Then just run right into an application.

The point is YOU don't have to answer this call. In fact, it's best if you don't because half the time the question isn't one you should be answering in the first place AND you should be out making that phone ring in the first place.

Loan Partner Takes the Call

- VIP front of the line script
- Takes a complete application
- Pulls credits
- Runs DU if credit is good enough
- Request the required documents for the full approval with urgency

- Determines which program they think is best (but doesn't discuss with client)
- Pick a Green spot in the LO's calendar / Text LO new loan just came in
- Gives back loan officer to sell the program and rage
- Takes back after program and rate is sold
- Tuesday / Thursday 15 minute pipeline updates
- Delivers bad news
- Tells loan officer to go get another loan

After our assistant answers the phone and does the "front of the line" script, they take a complete application. They pull the credit. They run DU or LP, if the credit is strong enough. They request the required documents for full approval and let the client know it is extremely helpful during the consultation if the loan officer has all this information. I have them say something like,

> "We know how valuable your time is. To make sure that {LO Name} is fully prepared for your consultation, s/he needs to see your pay stubs, and a few bank statements so that we can discuss what options are best for you. Can you have those ready and emailed to me before your meeting?"

If they know how, they can structure the file for you and do some income calculations so you don't have to. They don't discuss this with the client—you will. It's just that they do some of the research and set up work.

They schedule a time for you to meet with the clients, whether face-to-face, on a phone call, or even a Zoom.us meeting to go over their loan docs. I like to do my consults in the afternoon so I can use my mornings to go out and get the business in the door.

Think about a doctor's office. A chart is fully prepared—the patient has filled out all the proper paperwork, then had his height, weight, temperature and blood pressure taken before the doctor even walks in the exam room. Someone else has taken a full medical/drug history and has asked the reason for their visit. The doctor only needs 10–15 minutes to make a diagnosis and then hands the file back off to his nurse. This is a great model for your mortgage practice.

Someone else takes the application, collects some initial documentation and structures the loan (if they know how). You verify the information, making sure that income, DTI's and credit were analyzed properly, and then you sell the loan to the client. Once you have a commitment from the borrower, you hand it back to the loan partner who gets it ready for processing. This allows you to live by a calendar. (Remember, you're like a DOCTOR—you work by appointment only!!!)

Eventually, as you grow, you may need to bring in a mortgage expert (a "doctor") who can replace you. I find this happens when you hit the 25–30 loans a month mark. This will allow you to spend more time out in the field selling and bringing in more business in.

Mistakes should be minimal with this system when everyone is doing their job and the mortgage expert is indeed an expert.

ı ꞇınd a short 15 minute meeting a day with your assistants / team keeps everyone on the same page and the loans moving forward. During those meetings, I like to ask three things,

1. What leads came in yesterday and where are we with those leads?
2. What loans are closing in the next week and are any "stuck" and what do we need to do about it? And finally,
3. Are there any problems I need to be aware of before I start calling my referral partners?"

Note: I'm not looking to solve those problems—I just want to be aware of them so I am not blindsided when I call my partners. My team solves those problems. If they can't solve those problems, I may not have the right people on my team.

Loan Partner

- Get loan into processing
- Gather required documents
- Babysit clients to keep the ball rolling
- Update clients every Tuesday on loan status
- Ask for business every Tuesday
  - 1–2 referrals for every 10 in process by just asking
- Clear all LO conditions

"Just Ask"

I have found the best way to get more loans in the door is to ask people I am already doing business with for a referral. Each

Tuesday, we call EVERYONE involved with loans in process a1 ask them for a referral (both agents, both borrowers, the title agent, the insurance agent and anyone else we can think of). If you are closing 10 loans or less, you should make these calls yourself. After all, these are sales calls. Any more volume than that and you may want to have someone else help out.

I do like to have a "reason" for my call. Here are a couple of ideas you can use to "break the ice."

Ice Breaker #1

Call the customer and give them an update on where their loan is in the process. This is a 30-second update! Why? Because the purpose of the call is to ask for business. Once you have given the update, finish with,

> *"Well I don't want to keep you. I know you're busy. But before I let you go, is there anyone else that you know that could use our help with a mortgage? Referrals are the backbone of my business and the primary way I bring in new business. Is there anyone that you can think of?"* Most likely they will not have a name right then. Our response will be, *"That's OK. Can I ask you a huge favor? When a friend, family member, or co-worker is looking to buy, sell, or refinance, can I count on you to give me a call?"*

If your CRM or LOs do this update for you, that's great! Use Ice Breaker #2 only when they aren't getting updates any other way. I don't like it because it requires I know what's happening f things aren't going smooth, I might be tempted

in where it doesn't belong, which takes me away

Ice Breaker #2

I still call every Tuesday, but I have fun tips I give out instead. As before, I always ask for the business at the end of the call. Here is a multi-week approach to this Ice Breaker strategy.

Week One—Welcome call and ask if the customer has set up their mover yet. Remind them to get this done so they aren't left scrambling at the end.

Week Two—Remind the customer we will be doing a secondary Verification of Employment (VOE) and credit check so don't buy crap and don't quit their job! (Say this really nicely. LOL)

Week Three—You can do a half-way survey at this point… something like, *"How's my team doing? Our goal is to get a 5-star review."* Or you can ask if they have their utilities taken care of in preparation for their move.

Week Four—Let them know what they need to do for the closing or, if you've closed, ask for the 5-star review. *"Is there anything that would prevent you from giving us a 5-star review? If I send you a link, do you think you could take five minutes to fill it out and get it back to us by tomorrow?"*

At the end of every call, finish with,

> *"Well I don't want to keep you. I know you're busy. But before I let you go, is there anyone else that you know that could use our help with a mortgage? Referrals are the backbone of my business and the primary way I bring in new business. Is there anyone that you can think of?" Most likely they will not have a name right then. Your response will be, "That's OK. Can I ask you a huge favor? If you think of anyone, can I count on you to give me a call?"*

The Hardest Parts for Loan Officers

This process does bring up some challenges for LOs sometimes. Here is a short list.

Hardest Part

- Loan officer letting go
- Trusting your loan partner
- Being ok with your free time
- Putting on your war paint
- Make sure to do money making activities every day
- Break the system (Jack Roush)
- The #1 fear
- You are worthy of so much more, my friend!

By far, the hardest part for most loan officers in all this is just to let go and let their team take care of things. Here's some breaking news: if your team consistently drops the ball, maybe you've got the wrong team. Enough said.

Another thing that's hard for loan officers is being okay with their free time. They're used to working 24/7 and, when they get a little downtime, they're not sure what to do with it. You've got to have some white space in your life. You've got to have some time to recharge your batteries and get in creative mode. My best ideas don't come when I'm sitting here in the office. My best ideas come when I'm out riding my motorcycle or sitting on the beach with my family or going for a hike up in the mountains or when walking the streets of Europe. It's during the downtime new ideas just come to my head.

When you're in the office, you're too busy thinking about what you have to do next, what you've got to get done, where you need to network, etc. You can't grow your business that way because you're too busy "in" your business. We have all heard that old adage that you have to work ON your business, not IN your business. You can only do that if you have down time in your day, right?

So, Monday thru Friday from 9am–5pm, you are going to do what I call "putting on your war paint." I'll talk more about this in Book 2. But let me give you a sneak peek… you are actually going to be doing it Monday through only Thursday!

For now, you want to make sure you're doing the money-making activities we talked about throughout this book—the A activities. At this point, here is the question that loan officers ask me:

"Carl, what if something goes wrong?"

First of all, something IS going to go wrong and that's okay. Put your black pants on and push forward. One of my favorite examples of this comes from NASCAR of all places!

Relentlessly Break Your Systems to Win

Jack Roush is a very famous NASCAR engine builder. He owns five different race teams in NASCAR. Many of the other race teams buy his engines for their cars to race against him. It's the weirdest thing ever… it's like buying the other team's quarterback to play on your team.

During an interview he was asked,

"Jack, what makes you so special? Why are your engines so much better than everyone else's?" And he said, "I grew up a trouble shooter. I was always tinkering and taking things apart. In fact, my dad said he couldn't wait for me to leave home so all his stuff would be left alone. My first big job was with Ford and it was to work on quality control. That taught me to always work on making things better! When I started building my own engines, we built the engine and then tested the heck out of it. We would run it till it blew up. Then we would tear it apart to see what broke. I'd then make the part better, stronger or faster. We'd put the engine back together, fire it up, and do it all again. And so, while everybody else is afraid of breaking the engine, here at Roush Industries, we encourage it. We embrace breakage because then I build a bigger, better, faster machine."

And I'm going to tell you the same thing. In your mortgage business with your team, break the system. Let it run. See what breaks. Maybe nothing will break but let it run and let's see if it does. If it does, fix that part and make it even better. Don't be afraid of mistakes—just learn from them.

Now you might say,

> *"wait a minute, Carl. I might lose a deal. I might even lose a referral partner."*

And I would say you are absolutely right. While none of us WANTS that to happen, you have to be okay losing that one deal so you can get the next ten deals. You have to break the system so you can build a bigger, better, faster, stronger machine. You have to be *willing* to break the system. That's how you build an epic mortgage business. If you aren't willing to fail sometimes, you will not get very far.

So, we've talked about letting go, trusting the team, being ok with some down time, and breaking the engine. Now let's address what I see as the number one fear of loan officers when they start building a team and handing things off. Many loan officers may think they will be seen as unnecessary. I'm here to tell you that's just not true.

You're the conductor of the orchestra. Without you waving the baton, there is no machine. Nothing works without you. It's okay. You don't have to mop the floors to be seen as important at the hotel you own—somebody else mops the floors. You don't have to be chasing conditions to be important in your mortgage business—somebody else does that. You do the most important part of all—you make the phone ring. That's where the money is. So just push through that and know you are so worthy of so much more.

Chapter 9

Summary and
Next Action Steps

One day when I was a young boy, I was in my grandmother's backyard in Crystal River, Florida. As we were playing, we looked up in a palm tree and saw a parrot that looked much like the one in this picture.

Now, this bird is not a native of Florida so we assumed it was someone's pet that had escaped. My grandmother looked over at me and said, *"I'm going to get me that bird."*

I thought grandma was crazy because she was waaayyy too old to climb that tree (She may have been 50 which is really YOUNG to me these days!!!)

But I played along and asked her, *"Grandma, how are you going to do that?"* She said, *"Quick—go in the garage and get one of my big empty bird cages."* So I ran over to the garage and grabbed the biggest cage I could find. It was about the same size as I was, as I remember it. She told me to put it at the base of the tree, open the door and step back.

I did what she said and she waved me to come over by her kind of out of sight. As we're standing there, it hit me. Grandma's crazy! Grandma thinks this bird is just going to magically fly into this cage. And I thought there's no way he's going to do that! He came from that cage and now he's living in freedom. There is no water, no food, no boy bird, no girl bird. There's just a cage and a stick. But in a matter of minutes, that bird flew right down to the ground, took one hop into that cage and then up on the stick!

Grandma walked over, shut the door and she held up the cage with a bird she named Harry. I was awestruck! So I asked, *"what just happened, Grandma? Why in the world did he fly into that cage?"* We both knew he had been in a cage before, had escaped and, up until one minute ago, was living a life of freedom.

She said,*"Carl, I'll tell you why that bird did that and I want you to think about this real good. He flew back in that cage because it was familiar and it's what he knew."*

I really didn't understand that story until many years later when I found myself in a cage, per se, with my own situation. That story popped into my head and, even though it was 40 years later, I suddenly knew exactly what my grandmother was talking about when she gave me that teaching.

The reason I'm sharing this story with you now is because I just finished mapping out with you how to build a team who will help free you up. When we remove reactive activity and do nothing but proactive activity—that number one thing that makes you most your money—you will have true freedom. And not just financial freedom, but time-wise and stress-wise as well.

But here is what is going to happen. You'll be in your office and say, *"Hey, I just read this great book and this guy talked about how you get a team and have them answer the phone and help take the applications and chase conditions so you can go out and close more loans and make more money and not work weekends or evenings."*

And I promise you a co-worker or manager is going to say, *"I've done that. I had an assistant one time. They screwed everything up. Worst thing that ever happened. Don't do that. If you want something done right, you gotta do it yourself. You need to chase the conditions all on your own, that's what loan officers are supposed to do."*

My question to you is this: what will you do when that happens? Will you listen to them or will you listen to your heart telling you there is a better way?

As I close out here, I'm just going to beg and plead with you— don't fly back in the cage.

This book has mapped out a life of freedom, showing you how to run a successful mortgage business, and how you can focus on the parts that you enjoy and have someone else help with the rest. Screw swallowing the frogs. Start doing only those things that make you more money, those things you actually enjoy doing and those things you have a knack for—don't go back in the cage! Choose to live your life with freedom.

Over the years, I've often thought about that bird flying into that cage so many years ago just so I could tell you this story to help you stay out of your "cage". I hope you accept the challenge.

Thank you so much for reading this book. I look forward to talking with you when you call in or attend one of our events.

To quickly summarize, we talked about getting B activities off your plate, so you could concentrate on A activities (proactive vs. reactive). We covered finding and training your team, the perfect loan flow process, fail-proof scripts that leverage your time for higher-paying activities and doing what you love.

I'm already planning my next book, where we will go into more detail regarding A activities. We will talk about upping your mindset and I'll share some advanced strategies I use with our private clients to help them grow their mortgage businesses.

Here's the last nugget I'll share in this book… your business grows only as fast as you do. And, clearly, you are ready for growth or you wouldn't be reading this book. So I encourage you to follow through on what you've learned here by taking action. If you need a little support, my team and I are here for you—we have your back. Just give us a call, text us, shout out on social media, send a smoke signal… something to let us know you want to keep your momentum going from reading this book.

Also, I would love to hear how things are going in your business. I want to know what you're doing that's working, and what's not working too. Your 'experiments' and outcomes, even when unexpected, in business can help others. Because let's face it—we're all just walking each other home. And I believe generous people generate.

So, share what you know and learn from everybody else too. Visit our website at **MortgageMarketingAnimals.com**, listen to a podcast at **LoanOfficerFreedom.com** or attend one of our events to connect with like-minded people and help you grow in your mortgage business.

Or, if you want to move to the front of the line and schedule your free one-on-one Zoom meeting to discuss the strategies in this book and map out a plan to close more loans while working less hours, so that you can achieve your freedom even faster, meet me right now at **LoanOfficerStrategyCall.com**. I'll see you there :-)

—Carl

P.S.: If this book brought up questions for you, great! Please share your questions, and your comments and takeaways, on our wall at: **Facebook.com/MortgageMarketingAnimals**—we'd love to know! (Who knows? You might inspire my next book!) :+)

The Freedom Club

The Most Powerful Group of Loan Officers in the World to Help You Get Better Clients, Close More Deals, Enhance Your Income

If you're a loan officer or Branch Manager closing eight loans a month or more, then The Freedom Club is for you. As a member, you'll receive all the awesome benefits of Mortgage Marketing Animals.

In addition, you will have access to our full library of scripts for every occasion; loan checklists, systems and processes; job descriptions and ads; tracking sheets for leads, prospects, closings, and conversion rates; employee manuals; advanced loan-getting strategies and more.

Mastermind retreats every 90–120 days with other top-producing members are also included. Most importantly, you will receive personalized, one-on-one accountability coaching every two weeks. Here a plan will be designed specifically around you, your team, your market and your goals for the future.

Want a sneak peek at what it means to be in The Freedom Club? Check it out here:

FreedomClubApplication.com

If you have any questions, just give us a call at **(727) 787-2275.**

The Mortgage Marketing Animals Connected

A Membership Group of Loan Officers Sharing Unbelievably Effective Marketing Strategies

We are a Mastermind Group of like-minded Loan Officers from across the country who research, share and implement an incredible collection of unbelievably effective marketing strategies.

We believe success breeds success and that we are at our best when we as a group are helping others to succeed.

We believe our collective success will far exceed our individual successes.

We believe success is dynamic. It does not stand still. Each of us is constantly becoming either more or less successful.

On its own, an ember cools and the heat it produces dies away. But, as part of a collection of other burning embers, the heat builds and provides warmth for those around it.

This is a members' only group—if you are not already a member, you can learn more here:

LoanOfficerStrategyCall.com

Check Out Carl's Podcast

Every week, Carl brings you the best and brightest in personal interviews to discover the keys to success that are working in the field. This podcast is dedicated to inspiring loan officers to take the best of what they know to help them create the business results and lifestyle they really want.

Carl's style is casual, down-to-earth and practical. He empowers listeners while entertaining them and sharing tools, stories and strategies that can accelerate their mortgage loan business results.

Check out the podcast here:

LoanOfficerFreedom.com/

And if you have a success strategy to share for the show, please call our office at **(727) 787-2275**—we'd love to hear it!

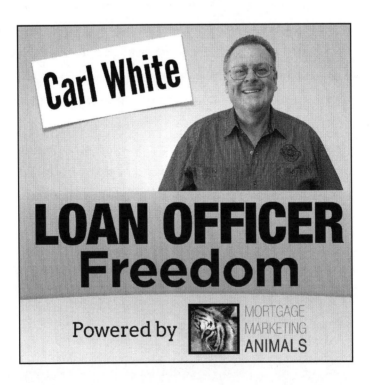

About Carl White

I am a husband, and a father to three wonderful young adults. My family and I enjoy boating, camping, and I am passionate about traveling the country on my Harley Davidson while masterminding with the top thought leaders in the world.

On the business side of things, I am the Founder/ Chief Strategist of The Mortgage Marketing Animals and also the host of the #1 Podcast for loan officers in America.

I first began my venture into the mortgage business as a loan officer in October of 1999. Within eight months of opening the doors at Family First Mortgage, I became the top-producing branch out of approximately 336 branches nationwide. I also began to train fellow loan officers in my "paint by numbers" approach. This technique helped the LO's retain more closings while working less hours in a week. Five years later, I opened my own mortgage business called Time Mortgage.

Who I Help

I help loan officers to implement proven marketing strategies I have personally used in my own career and had great success with, measured by hundreds of thousands of dollars in revenue each and every month. While I make no income claims for you (of course), it is my belief I may be able to help you increase yours.

How I Help

I show specific step-by-step instructions on how to drastically increase your monthly loan production and income while working only 32 hours per week. I do this by teaching loan officers to hyper-focus their efforts, and to stop doing wasteful activities they are currently doing that are not producing measurable results. By following the strategies I provide, my clients are able to regain the freedom to do the things they want to do. Worrying about when and where the next deal will come from is no longer a concern.

Specialties

Strategizing | Marketing | Advising | Speaking
Video Blogging | Marketing Seminars | Marketing Webinars
Generating Leads | Social Media Marketing | Video Marketing

Carl can be reached at:

Email: **carl.white@TheMarketingAnimals.com**

Phone: **727-787-2275**

Website: **MortgageMarketingAnimals.com/**

Facebook: **Facebook.com/MortgageMarketingAnimals**

LinkedIn: **LinkedIn.com/in/MarketingAnimals**

Podcast: **LoanOfficerFreedom.com/**

Instagram: **@themarketinganimals**

One Last Thing...

If you enjoyed this book or found it useful, I would be very grateful if you'd post a short review on Amazon. Your support really does make a difference. I read all the reviews personally to get your feedback and make this book even better.